The Spiritual Legacy
OF
JOHN FOSTER DULLES

The
Spiritual Legacy

OF

JOHN FOSTER

DULLES

SELECTIONS
FROM HIS ARTICLES AND ADDRESSES

◇◇◇◇

Edited with an Introduction by
HENRY P. VAN DUSEN

◇◇◇◇

Philadelphia
THE WESTMINSTER PRESS

LIBRARY OF CONGRESS CATALOG CARD NO. 60–8635

PRINTED IN THE UNITED STATES OF AMERICA

Contents

The President's Tribute

JOHN FOSTER DULLES is dead. A lifetime of labor for world peace has ended. His countrymen and all who believe in justice and the rule of law grieve at the passing from the earthly scene of one of the truly great men of our time.

Throughout his life, and particularly during his eventful six years as Secretary of State, his courage, his wisdom, and his friendly understanding were devoted to bettering relations among nations. He was a foe only to tyranny.

Because he believed in the dignity of men and in their brotherhood under God, he was an ardent supporter of their deepest hopes and aspirations. From his life and work, humanity will, in the years to come, gain renewed inspiration to work ever harder for the attainment of the goal of peace with justice. In the pursuit of that goal, he ignored every personal cost and sacrifice, however great.

We who were privileged to work with him have lost a dear and close friend as all Americans have lost a champion of freedom.

DWIGHT D. EISENHOWER

Gettysburg, Pa.
May 24, 1959

Preface

WHEN THIS VOLUME was first projected, it was expected that ten or a dozen items might be discovered that would merit inclusion. However, an examination of John Foster Dulles' files disclosed more than fifty addresses and articles concerned primarily with the moral and spiritual foundations of world order, the significance of religion, and the role of the churches. From these, the present selection has been made.

In speaking or writing on the same or closely related themes on different occasions and to different audiences over a period of twenty years, it was inevitable that Mr. Dulles should make some reiteration of emphases and even repetition of certain phrases, sentences, and quotations. In some instances, these have been omitted from the later sources, as have sections of material dealing with then current but now past issues. But for the most part, the articles and addresses stand as originally prepared.

Thanks are gratefully acknowledged to Mrs. Dulles and to Mr. Allen Dulles for fullest collaboration and assistance in the preparation of the collection, and also to Mr. Dulles' former secretary at the State Department, Miss Phyllis Bernau. Miss Barbara Griffis, librarian of the William Adams Brown

Ecumenical Library in Union Theological Seminary, has rendered invaluable help in tracking down sources and gathering items for inclusion. I am also indebted to the several publishers for permission freely given to reprint copyrighted materials.

H.P.V.D.

Union Theological Seminary
New York
February 12, 1960

Man of Faith

THE DEATH of John Foster Dulles on May 24, 1959, was the occasion of an outpouring of acclaim without precedent in our day unless for royalty or a chief of state. Not only throughout the length and breadth of his own country but across the world, tributes of admiration, of gratitude, almost of reverence, welled up from persons in every rank and station of life and of every outlook and allegiance. Veteran Washington taxi drivers declared that they could not recall crowds in such density as the tens of thousands who lined the route of his funeral cortege from the Episcopal Cathedral on Mount Saint Albans to Arlington Cemetery. Heads of Governments and of political parties who had often been his sharpest critics and most unyielding opponents vied with close associates and lifelong friends in the warmth and sincerity of their eulogies. It was universally recognized that his nation and the community of nations had lost one of the most gifted, dedicated, and influential statesmen of this century. No less frequent was the recognition that from history had passed a man of most unusual character.

Time and again, the question has been asked, not in idle curiosity but in eager desire to understand the secret of his greatness: What manner of man was he? How are we to interpret, if not explain, this remarkable person?

From time to time, columnists and correspondents who had had the opportunity of being much associated with Mr. Dulles have spoken of the human being they had discovered: a combination of qualities so contrasted as to seem almost contradictory—formidable yet touchingly gentle, aloof yet engagingly friendly, stern yet delightfully playful, solemn and yet heartily savoring authentic wit and humor.

His gifts of intellect were evident to all. As an undergraduate of Princeton University, they had placed him at the head of the graduating class. In middle life, they had brought him to pre-eminence in his chosen profession of the law. As Secretary of State, they won the respect of statesmen on both sides of every issue. No less obvious was an iron discipline of mind and habit and unyielding fixity of purpose. But behind both intellect and will was a profounder center and source of strength.

No one who had the privilege of Mr. Dulles' intimate confidence could for one moment be in doubt as to the key to the person who harbored such contrasting qualities, as to the deeper springs of his character, or as to the secret of its strength and its endurance. "Man of faith," he has often been called. But "faith" is a weather-worn word of a hundred variant meanings, and for many, rather hackneyed and uncongenial associations.

"Man of Christian faith"—there is the bedrock without which everything else that might be said about him is incomplete, indeed inexplicable.

It was formed—that character—in a Presbyterian manse in Watertown, New York, in attendance four times each Sunday at church worship and Sabbath school, and around the family piano through the singing of hymns that, as many would testify, can form the substratum of personality almost as decisively as overt instruction or formal worship. The imprint of those early associations was deeply implanted upon his convictions and his character, as he himself repeatedly bore witness in later years. It was no accident that, in his last days when suffering sharpened and the inescapable end threatened, he longed to hear again the hymns that had nourished his spirit in youth and across the years—not sentimental modern hymns but the grand old affirmations of faith: "The Spacious Firmament on High"; "When Morning Gilds the Skies"; "God of Our Life, Through All the Circling Years"; "Work, for the Night Is Coming"; All Praise to Thee, My God, This Night"; and especially the hymn beginning, "Through the night of doubt and sorrow onward goes the pilgrim band," for this last was, not only by expressed preference but also by inherent sympathy, John Foster Dulles' favorite hymn. And so a recording of these hymns was made and, night by night, the waning spirit was rekindled by the great hymns of Christian faith.

A dozen years ago, returning from a conference of the Churches' Commission to Study the Bases of a Just and Durable Peace over which Mr. Dulles had presided and to which he had lured some of his skeptical colleagues from the world of affairs, one of these close friends turned to him and chided playfully: "Foster, your mother must have been terribly disappointed when you didn't become a minister." The stern jaw stiffened, and that familiar granite voice blurted sharply, almost rudely: "Nearly broke her heart."

As a matter of fact, his mother rejoiced in his achievements as lawyer and statesman. In any event, the maternal hope was not defeated. He who might have been a powerful preacher of the Christian gospel became a pre-eminent pioneer in a Christian vocation, rarer and perhaps far more needful than professional clergy—the lay ministry, fulfilling one of the central and greatly neglected ideals of the Calvinist tradition in which Mr. Dulles had been reared: "Every profession, a sacred calling; every Christian, a minister of Christ."

Plato defined the ideal state—when "statesmen should be philosophers" and "philosophers, statesmen." Christianity envisions a loftier and more demanding conception of public leadership: the minister of state—a minister of Christ in his sacred calling. It is difficult to name anyone in our day who has more fully discharged that high vocation.

How firmly the truths of Christian faith had established themselves within Mr. Dulles' securest certainties was disclosed by the words to which he habitually had recourse, especially in moments of special intensity, in speech of climactic importance.

A study of John Foster Dulles' vocabulary, particularly at those times when he was speaking from central conviction and to the crucial point, discovers a single phrase occurring over and over again like a reiterated refrain: "a *righteous* and *dynamic faith.*" Each of the three words was carefully chosen; each is essential to the whole.

"*Righteous.*" A passion for justice, for righteousness impregnating the affairs of men, the affairs of state. "Too much these days," he declared, "we forget that men's ability to control the physical depends upon the moral. Nothing that statesmen can contrive will work if it does not reflect the moral conscience of the time. Whenever that limitation is ignored, failure ensues." Moralism, he was sometimes accused of; so far as I know, he never denied the charge. To have done so would have been to repudiate a basic certitude: the moral order, a divine order, the will of God—by which the decisions of statesmen must ultimately be judged, into conformity with which the relations of peoples, as of persons, must finally be brought.

"*Dynamic.*" Another of his great, recurring words, demanding a "dynamic peace," in the conviction of the living, moving, ever-changing character of the divine order for human life with its openness to change, its hopefulness toward a better ordering of society. Dynamic—the very temper of the pilgrim.

"*Faith.*" "Righteous" and "dynamic"—these are the adjectives. But "faith" is the noun, which the adjectives identify and which alone can translate them into reality. To this we shall return.

The springs of character are revealed, not only in the words to which men habitually have recourse, but—far more—in their spontaneous *actions,* sometimes trivial as the world measures importance.

One such incident, doubtless representative of many, may now be disclosed. A very minor official in our foreign service was threatened with dishonorable dismissal and disgrace on charges of subversion, one of many victims of the witch hunt directed by Senator McCarthy and his lieutenants. The man laid his case before a friend of Mr. Dulles', who became convinced of his innocence and brought the matter to Mr. Dulles' attention.

The young man had already been condemned, deprived of appointment and salary, and his appeal had been denied by a loyalty board and the Undersecretary. Only direct intervention by the Secretary of State could save him. At the time, Mr. Dulles was in the midst of pressing affairs—journeying to Europe, to Asia, to South America. But he personally reviewed the voluminous record, overrode the loyalty board and his Undersecretary, ordered exoneration and honorable restitution leading to appointment to a much more responsible post. Reporting his decision to the friend who had ventured to trouble him with so small a matter, he wrote:

"The final papers in D——'s case have now come before me. I know that you will be pleased to learn that on the basis of convincing evidence I have given him a full and complete clearance.

"Thank you again for writing me about this matter."

The career of a minor subordinate was salvaged, his honor vindicated. This was the concrete action of a man of faith—"righteous and dynamic faith."

From his own clear view of the practical and active faith demanded of Christians sprang his impatience with the churches that caused him to hold somewhat aloof from them in middle life. He was alienated by what he considered their disregard of, and disloyalty to, the mind of Christ. In 1937 he wrote:

"I am a layman, of Christian upbringing. Despite the fact that my beliefs are somewhat diluted, I have always assumed, as a matter of course, that it was the Christian churches which could be looked to, to lift mankind from those morasses of which the underlying cause is usually moral decay. But recently, I had begun to doubt. The churches had lost those

qualities which in the past had made them formidable. . . .
The church, it seemed, had become 'soft.' . . . Church membership had ceased to be synonymous with dangerous and
difficult living for a high ideal. . . . The church as institution-
alized by man . . . had too much devoted itself to vain repetitions and too little to doing the Father's will."

However, when World War II lowered and then broke,
and Mr. Dulles' abilities and energies were given almost
wholly to the furtherance of a "just and durable peace," he
found himself drawn into a new appreciation of the churches
as effective allies through their generation of a righteous and
dynamic faith. He declared:

"The churches are peculiarly qualified to promote a solution of the kind of problems which today vex mankind. . . .
The Christian churches are powerful for good in so far as
they propagate spiritual truth. . . . They are unique in their
combined qualifications. . . . Only through an approach of
such universality is there any promise of a solution."

It was in this conviction that he consented, somewhat re-
luctantly, to serve on the Board of Directors of Union Theological Seminary, and did so from 1945 until he left for
Washington in 1953. His only query was, "What do you
want me to do?" For he disdained nominal memberships; he
was impatient with perfunctory meetings or inactive service.
He felt that time was too precious, the issues of our day too
urgent, to permit anything less than vigorous and sustained
effort in behalf of whatever responsibility one accepted.

It was as a convinced and active churchman, more particularly as Chairman of the Commission to Study the Bases of a Just and Durable Peace, that Mr. Dulles was led to re-examine and rethink his own convictions on the nature and content of Christian faith, especially in their bearing upon the issues of peace and world order, which were his central concern. It was in that context that he formulated and gave expression to the great bulk of writings and utterances that constitute the substance of this collection, whether they were addressed to church groups or to a great variety of secular audiences—the readers of *Life* magazine, the Missouri Bar Association, the graduates of the War College, many national radio audiences.

It is not difficult to identify the structure of Christian conviction that determined his own attitude toward public affairs, which though Christian in origin he felt to be of universal authority, which he believed to be of the essence of the American tradition, and which he sought to have laid as the foundation principles of world order. Those convictions ring, like a determinative motif, through all his speeches and writings:

1. *The reality and regnancy of moral law, of moral principle and moral structure undergirding and ultimately conforming the affairs of nations, the relations of peoples no less than of persons.* "The moral law, happily, is a universal law. It is reflected by many great religions. . . . That fact is of immense value. It is why, even today, moral concepts can have world-wide influence."

2. *The divine endowment of human beings as children of God, made in his image and endowed by him with certain inalienable rights.* "Since those rights are given by God, no men,

however powerful or however numerous, can rightfully take them away from other men, even though those others be only weak or few."

3. *The authority and practicability of the teachings of Jesus.* He spoke often of the ethical precepts of Jesus. He regarded them, not as counsels of perfection with authority solely upon religious devotees or as specifications for some transworldly Kingdom, but as guiding principles for daily life and practice here and now, not only of individuals, but also of communities and the world community. He believed that Christ gives and expects, in particular, four indispensable qualities: vision, compassion, clarity of mind, action.

"Christ wanted men to see, to see far and to see truly. To get that kind of vision, he pointed out, requires avoidance of hypocrisies and group prejudices, which distort the vision and make men imagine they see what is not really there.

"Christ wanted men to have hearts that comprehend the human significance of what is seen. That kind of heart requires, he pointed out, avoidance of material self-seeking, which makes men hard and indifferent to all that cannot serve their selfish ends.

"Christ wanted men to reason clearly and serenely. That requires, he pointed out, avoidance of evil emotions, such as hatred and vengefulness, which enflame men's minds and distract them from the real problems that confront them.

"Christ wanted men to act."

4. *The obligation to action.* "Finally, we must act. Christ did not teach a purely contemplative religion. 'Go' and 'do' were his constant injunction. 'Let your light so shine before men that they may see your good works.'"

5. *The necessity of faith*. One cannot fail to be struck by
the fact that, taken together, these five convictions embody
the very heart of the Judaeo-Christian faith, from the teaching
regarding man's creation in Genesis, through the insistence
upon the divine ordering of society in the great prophets, and
the pivotal authority of the mind of Christ and his reiterated
emphasis upon deeds no less than belief, to the climactic stress
upon faith in Paul and the author of The Letter to the Hebrews, although there is no evidence that Mr. Dulles himself
was aware of the comprehensiveness of his interpretation of
Christian certitude.

The final emphasis falls on *faith,* and returns us to the note
with which we began.

However, we have said, "faith" is a weather-worn word
with countless meanings, and for many, vague and somewhat
hackneyed associations. One always recalls the lad who replied to his Sunday school questionnaire, What is faith? with
"Faith is believing what you know ain't true!" Despite its
manifold uses, in Christian understanding faith always carries
a twofold connotation: It speaks of convictions believed to be
true but never fully proved true—"certainty of things not
seen." But, in another and less recognized sense, faith denotes
action; it is life devotion to ends, to ideals that are held to be
sound and realizable but are never wholly realized—"assurance
of things hoped for." So, in the classic exposition of Christian
faith in the eleventh chapter of The Letter to the Hebrews, to
which Mr. Dulles himself reverted over and over again—the
catalog of the figures of faith, the chronicle of the pilgrims of
faith—the emphasis throughout is upon action: "Abraham,
when he was called, went, not knowing whither." . . . "Noah
built." . . . Others "conquered kingdoms, enforced justice,

won strength out of weakness." Yes, and "these all died in faith, not having received the promises, but having seen them afar off."

If it be asked, How is such faith with its practical fruit in action born and nurtured and sustained within the human spirit?, this is the answer: It has its basis in that other side of faith which we more familiarly associate with the word. Faith *is* devotion to ends believed to be achievable but never fully achieved. Such life devotion is possible because faith is also and more fundamentally trust in certainties felt to be true but never wholly proved true: certainty that truth alone permanently prevails, that right does ultimately triumph, certainty of God.

If one were to associate a single Biblical passage with Mr. Dulles' life, there could be little hesitancy in its choice— Heb., ch. 11, his own most-quoted chapter of Scripture. And, from the literature of Christianity down through the centuries might be chosen those words in *The Pilgrim's Progress* describing the journey of Valiant-for-truth which were so appropriately spoken at his funeral.

In that catalog of the pioneers of faith, John Foster Dulles takes his rightful place; in that chronicle his struggles for a better world, for a just and lasting peace, are to be entered: man of faith, man of Christian faith—a righteous and dynamic faith.

So it was altogether in character that toward the last his spirit should turn to "Through the Night of Doubt and Sorrow" and that as his mortal body was borne up the slopes of Arlington Cemetery to its last resting place the strains that greeted his funeral cortege should have been those of the triumphant words of his best-loved hymn:

"Through the night of doubt and sorrow
    Onward goes the pilgrim band,
Singing songs of expectation,
    Marching to the promised land.
One the object of our journey,
    One the faith which never tires,
One the earnest looking forward,
    One the hope our God inspires."

I

The Faith of a Statesman

At the time of John Foster Dulles' birth on February 25, 1888, his family were making their home in Watertown, New York, where his father, Rev. Allen Macy Dulles, had been called the previous year to the pastorate of the First Presbyterian Church. There they lived until 1904, the year in which Foster left home to enter Princeton University and Dr. Dulles became Professor of Theism and Apologetics in Auburn Theological Seminary, Auburn, New York. It was in Watertown and its environs, near the southern shore of Lake Ontario, in the church of which his father was minister and the home over which he presided, that the years of infancy, boyhood, and youth were spent. It was during those years that the physique, the mental outlook, and the spirit were molded by forces of whose formative influence upon him Foster was deeply conscious. It was on a small island off the southern shore of Lake Ontario not far from Watertown that he and his wife built the roughhewn camp where they sought retreat from the pressures of public life and found physical and spiritual reinvigoration.

Twice during the last decade of his life, Foster Dulles returned to the church of his childhood to speak from the pulpit where his father had preached throughout his boyhood. The first of these addresses is perhaps the most frankly autobiographical and revealing self-disclosure that he ever uttered. In it are summarized many of the convictions that infused all he said and did. The second address in the Watertown church, one of his last public statements on religion and morals, concludes this volume.

Mr. Dulles referred frequently to the Conference on "Church, Community, and State" at Oxford in July, 1937, which he attended as one of the American delegates. It was there that he first became convinced of the potential influence of the churches as effective forces for the advance of peace and peaceful change—a reversal of his previous attitude that may, not unfairly, be described as a "conversion," an about-face. The second paper in this section is an interpretation of that conference; the third reiterates its profound effect upon him.

It was in his negotiation of the peace treaty with Japan in 1951 that Mr. Dulles felt that he had the most significant opportunity actually to test in practice the moral principles for international order to which he was committed. This attempt is set forth in personal terms in the fourth selection.

John Foster Dulles was born in the home in Washington, D.C., of the grandfather whose name he was to bear, John W. Foster, then Secretary of State in the Grover Cleveland administration. In June, 1955, he was invited to give the baccalaureate address and receive an honorary degree from Indiana University on the one hundredth anniversary of his grandfather's graduation and the fiftieth anniversary of his honorary degree from his Alma Mater. This was the occasion for another declaration of Foster Dulles' personal faith, this time with special emphasis upon the American tradition. It supplies an appropriate transition to the next section of selections on "The American Heritage."

1

Faith of Our Fathers

To you who listen, this is just another Sunday. To me, it is an eventful day. This is the pulpit from which my father preached for many years, and from which he radiated an influence that is still felt here and elsewhere. Before me is the pew where I sat as a boy, little dreaming that this day would come when I would be speaking from his pulpit.

Those were times when Sunday was really set apart as God's day. There were then three church services — morning, afternoon, and evening — and Sunday school besides. The minister's family regularly attended all four services. Also, on each Sunday, we memorized about ten verses from The Psalms or the New Testament and in addition two verses of a hymn. Sunday then was a holy day, but hardly one of rest.

I cannot say that my mind never wandered during the church services. During the morning service there was the distracting prospect of licking the dasher with which I was to freeze the Sunday dinner ice cream. And during the afternoon service my thoughts returned to the woods and fields which I had roamed while bird-watching the Saturday before. But by the time I left Watertown in my seventeenth

Address at the First Presbyterian Church, Watertown, New York, Sunday, August 28, 1949.

year I had accumulated a considerable knowledge of the Bible and of Christian writings.

During the same time, I had developed a great interest in international affairs. That came from my grandfather, John W. Foster, who used to spend his summers in these parts and with whom I used to fish regularly at Henderson Harbor. As we sat together in a fishing skiff he would tell me of his diplomatic experiences in Mexico, Russia, Spain, and China. Also, he told of his experiences as a soldier in the Civil War — experiences that made him hate war and devote himself to the cause of peace. It became my ambition to go forward in that way.

I started as law clerk in an international law firm and came to work on many international problems and to attend many international conferences. During that period it did not seem to me that what I had learned here in church had much to do with the practical problems of war and peace. That was indeed my state of mind for thirty years, from 1907 when I attended with my grandfather the Second Hague Peace Conference, until 1937. In that year I presided at an international conference held at Paris under the auspices of the League of Nations, and then went on to attend the Oxford Conference on Church and State. That was a great Christian conference, with representatives of almost all the nations and all the races of the world. We discussed there the same critical problems that diplomats were discussing futilely at the League of Nations. But at Oxford we approached those problems with the guidance of a common standard — the moral law as revealed by Jesus Christ; and we dealt with each other as brothers, irrespective of national or racial differences. Under those conditions we could see how to solve problems that could not be solved in the distrustful atmosphere of national competition.

Then I began to understand the profound significance of the spiritual values that my father and mother had taught, and by which they had lived, here at Watertown. From then on I began to work closely with religious groups — Protestant, Catholic, and Jewish — for I had come to believe that, of all groups, they could make the greatest contribution to world order. Most of all I worked with the Commission on a Just and Durable Peace of the Federal Council of the Churches of Christ in America. During these same years I helped organize the United Nations and attended its meetings and those of the Council of Foreign Ministers. Serving at the same time in both religious and political groups made ever clearer the relationship between the two. I saw that there could be no just and durable peace except as men held in common certain simple and elementary religious beliefs: belief that there is a God, that he is the author of a moral law which they can know, and that he imparts to each human being a spiritual dignity and worth which all others should respect. Wherever these elementary truths are widely rejected, there is both spiritual and social disorder.

That fact is illustrated by fascism and communism. These are, in the main, atheistic and antireligious creeds. Orthodox Communists believe that there is neither God nor moral law, that there is no such thing as universal and equal justice, and that human beings are without soul or sacred personality. They are free of the moral restraints and compulsions which prevail in a religious society, and they think it quite right to use force and violence to make their way prevail.

In Russia, Communists have designed a form of society which they call "the dictatorship of the proletariat." They believe that their mission is to press all mankind into that precise mold and to do so by any and all means available.

Communists are, of course, entitled to have their own belief as to what is best for men, and they are entitled to try peacefully to bring their ideals into reality. That is the privilege of every human being. But since there is a God, since there is a moral law, since human personality is sacred, no human rulers can rightly use ruthless and violent methods and pitilessly crush all within their power who do not conform to their particular dictation.

At the first session of the United Nations Assembly at London, Mr. Vishinsky spoke about refugees — poor, wretched creatures who had fled Russia to escape liquidation. In words that were powered with deep hatred, and that struck like bullets from a machine gun, Mr. Vishinsky proclaimed the resolve of the Soviet Government to scour the face of the earth to find these refugees, to seize them and bring them back.

It was a cruel and frightening speech. It typified the fanaticism of Soviet Communism and its total denial of tolerance toward any who disagreed. Terrorism, which breaks men's spirits, is, to Communists, a normal way to make their creed prevail, and to them it seems legitimate because they do not think of human beings as being brothers through the Fatherhood of God.

If communism and fascism are hateful because of the consequences of their godlessness, it is equally true that they can be successfully resisted only by societies imbued with strong spiritual convictions. In Washington these days Congress is working on great plans to halt Communism by giving economic and military aid to those who, we hope, will resist. It is, however, perfectly clear that these plans will not succeed if they merely put material things into the hands of men who do not have a spiritual faith and who do not feel a sense of human brotherhood and of social responsibility. . . .

◇◇◇◇

[Here Mr. Dulles dealt in some detail with specific issues that at that time were to the fore.]

◇◇◇◇

Napoleon said that in time of war the moral is to the material as three is to one. I suppose that, in waging peace, the ratio is at least as high. We are apt to forget that and to think that the struggle in which we are now engaged can be won by material things alone. That is totally wrong. Wherever one looks around the world, one sees disorder that can be cured only by drawing on sources of moral power.

The Western democracies have had great prestige and authority in the world. That is because their practices developed under the dominating influence of religious beliefs. Their laws came, more and more, to protect the individual and to provide more equal justice. They found ways for bringing about social improvements peacefully, without class wars or the crushing of the weaker by the stronger. They encouraged men to develop their individual talents and to experiment along diverse and competitive lines of their own choosing. Under those stimulating conditions there developed material, intellectual, and spiritual richness; and to some degree at least that richness was shared with other peoples of the world. For one thousand years Western civilization grew in power and influence and was not seriously challenged. There was such a challenge by Islam one thousand years ago, and now we have the challenge of Soviet Communism. Whether or not we peacefully surmount the present challenge depends on basic things and most of all on whether our people love the Lord their God and their neighbors, and act accordingly.

The hope of America and the hope of the world does not lie

in our economic and military might. We have a duty to be materially strong and to share that strength with others who are in peril. But that is only a defensive, holding operation. The role of material power, as Admiral Mahan said, is to give moral ideals the opportunity to take root. Our basic strength is our capacity to propagate these moral ideals which must prevail if there is to be peace and justice in the world.

I am not, of course, suggesting that men and women should become Christians because that is the way for them to get peace. Such an argument would reverse the proper order of values. What I do say is that those who are Christians should see more clearly the possibilities that reside in the life and work of the churches.

There are millions in the world who want to do something for peace. They know the indescribable horror that another war would be, and they are eager to dedicate themselves to the preservation, in peace, of the freedoms that are our heritage. They are quite willing to give time and money to attain those ends. Many of them feel frustrated because they cannot find a channel through which to work. I suppose that, in sum total, thousands have asked me personally to suggest what they might do to help the cause of peace. Many in their worthy zeal become faddists, joining organizations that would stop war by paper slogans. After the First World War many of our finest people sought to end war by working for a treaty that would, as they put it, "outlaw war." They got what they asked for in the form of the Kellogg-Briand Pact, but it did not stop World War II by a single day. Many today are engaged in similar futilities. It is tragic that so much good intention goes for naught.

Men and women who have spiritual faith and who want also to do something practical to preserve peace and to meet the challenge of communism have, in their local church, the most effective medium that exists. It is the churches that dependably keep alive and pass on, from generation to generation, belief in God, in moral law, and in the spiritual nature of man. It is the churches that provide recruitment for the ministry. It is the churches that have missionary affiliations that spread great spiritual truths throughout the world. They have central agencies . . . that provide studies of world problems by qualified Christian statesmen. These, if used, can create an enlightened public opinion that will directly influence the acts of government and of the United Nations. That has been proved. Yet, today, such studies barely trickle into local congregations.

Many who are zealous for peace seem to feel that all this is remote from reality. They want a more direct and obvious role.

That mood will never bring lasting peace. Peace is won, as victory is won, by cumulative efforts, no one of which alone is decisive. In time of war men and women labor in munition plants and feel that they are contributing to victory; and so they are, although no single effort appreciably affects the outcome. But the outcome would be defeat if no one worked unless he was confident that the bullet he made would kill an enemy general.

The struggle for peace will never be won without the cumulative efforts of millions of individuals working in ways that develop moral power and organize it as mobile force. If believers would direct their zeal for peace more into church and missionary channels, the prospect of war would steadily recede.

Today our nation is relying greatly on material and military might. That is dangerous. A nation that possesses a great military establishment is apt to be influenced by the counsel of persons who believe in the inevitability of war or who believe that good ends can be gained by violent means. Our present course skirts, dangerously, the road to war. Our leaders take that risk because they feel that there is no adequate alternative. Policy makers work with the tools that, it seems, can be made available. Economic and military power can be developed under the spur of laws and appropriations. But moral power does not derive from any act of Congress. It depends on the relations of a people to their God. It is the churches to which we must look to develop the resources for the great moral offensive that is required to make human rights secure and to win a just and lasting peace.

Nearly two thousand years ago Christ said, "The truth shall make you free." Every one of the intervening years sustains that utterance. We meet here beneath a spire that points upward. That is symbolic. It points to the power above us from which we derive our spiritual strength, and it marks this building as the place where men can gather and draw that strength which alone enables those on earth to have the power to be free.

2

As Seen by a Layman

Large conferences are usually to be avoided. Intellectual advancement is apt to be in inverse ratio to the number of those participating therein. And while the massing of human beings facilitates the generation of emotion, that is a quality with which we are today surfeited. Nevertheless, I attended the Oxford Conference because it seemed to me that I might there find the answer to certain questions which perplexed me.

I am a layman, of Christian upbringing. Despite the fact that my beliefs are somewhat diluted, I have always assumed, as a matter of course, that it was the Christian churches which could be looked to, to lift mankind from those morasses of which the underlying cause is usually moral decay. But recently I had begun to doubt.

At few times in history have human needs been so great as during recent years. The world war had destroyed material and spiritual values to a degree which has only gradually been appreciated. Every country faced a long period of readjustment which tried the souls of men. It was obvious

An interpretation of the Oxford Conference on "Church, Community, and State," July 12–26, 1937. *Religion in Life*, Winter, 1938. Copyright, 1937, by Abingdon Press.

that the situation called for some constructive and directive force, based upon recognition of a common need rather than merely that of self or community or even nation. Instead of this, in international affairs those nations which were dominant sought to perpetuate for themselves a monopoly of the advantages which they had derived from the successful prosecution of power politics. Those nations which felt themselves wrongfully disadvantaged sought to redress the balance at the expense of others still weaker. Within the state, class warfare was waged in the effort of some to obtain, and of others, to retain, such relatively small amounts of accumulated wealth as existed in transferable form. All of this occurred in states which were nominally Christian and where public opinion was dominated, and public leadership exercised, by those who were members of Christian churches.

Deep troubles usually produce a new order of thinking. Thus, in certain areas there emerged new political and spiritual conceptions. The "state" was personified, even deified, as the sole source of human salvation. To the state's chosen objectives all else was to be subordinated, including the privilege of individual judgment and action. The state not only claimed complete allegiance but demanded of its followers those Spartan qualities necessary to make them most useful in the state's scheme of things.

These new creeds promptly came into conflict with the church. In retrospect we can see that this was inevitable. Nevertheless, at the time the conflict took us rather by surprise. We could look back over a record of centuries throughout which the church had successfully maintained its right to teach allegiance to Christ as superior to any secular loyalty. At many times the struggle had been bitter and had entailed heavy sacrifice. But the church had historically shown such

vitality in defense of this principle that it came to be assumed
that politicians would never again find it expedient to challenge the church upon this issue.

However, as is usually the case, it is when we feel most
secure that the greatest danger is present. It had doubtless
become apparent to any astute observer that the churches had
lost those qualities which in the past had made them formidable. No religion can survive which does not demand and
receive sacrifice from its adherents. Sacrifice is not only the
measure of loyalty but itself induces loyalty. We believe
intensely only in those causes to which we have contributed
of ourselves. But the churches, it seemed, had become "soft."
It had become conventional and even socially and materially
advantageous to become an enrolled Christian. No risk and
no sacrifice were involved. Church membership had ceased
to be synonymous with dangerous and difficult living for a
high ideal. This inspiring concept had been dropped by the
wayside for others to take up and incorporate in their own
authoritarian programs. Christianity was thus fought with
weapons abandoned by it from its own armory. In the result-
ant struggle, the churches in many countries were pushed
aside with surprising ease.

In the face of such occurrences it is not, I think, surprising
that many should have lost confidence in the church as insti-
tutionalized by man. Its weakness and ineffectiveness seemed
to prove that it had too much devoted itself to vain repetitions
and too little to doing the Father's will. . . .

◇◇◇◇

It was under such circumstances that the Oxford Conference
was held. It was attended by delegates from practically all of
the Christian churches except the Roman Catholic Church,
but including the Greek Orthodox Church. The delegates,

numbering some four hundred, were drawn from virtually every land and race and represented all shades of political opinion.

It is not my purpose here to summarize or to review the reports themselves. To some extent, as was inevitable, the reports are platitudinous; to some extent there were concessions to expediency in that words were chosen with a view to covering up differences which developed. To a considerable extent the reports devote themselves to condemning admitted evils. In this respect they are without particular value. It is easy to wax eloquent in denunciation of war and social injustice. But the danger of pursuing this course is that too often those who denounce feel that they have thereby fully discharged their duty.

But if the reports show evidence of human frailties, they are nonetheless documents of profound significance. Each of them contains an analysis, which is both intelligent and realistic, of great problems which today face the world. Each suggests, in relation thereto, a concrete and constructive approach which, if sincerely adopted by Christians, would go far to make possible a solution.

I illustrate by reference to the report of the Fifth Section dealing with international relations. The report goes deeper than a facile denunciation of war and eulogy of peace. It develops the fact that where, within a country, domestic tranquillity is on a firm basis, this is only because of the existence of a superior force — government — which is able and disposed, by new legislation, to adapt from time to time the social structure to changing social needs. In the world of nations no superior political agency exists. This means that change, which is always inevitable, can occur only through force or the voluntary action of the nations. "It therefore particularly devolves upon Christians to devote themselves to securing by voluntary action of their nations such changes in the international order as are from time to time required to avoid injustice and to permit equality of opportunity for individuals throughout the world. . . . The unequal distribution of natural advantages is one of the causes of war, if control is used to create a monopoly of national advantage. Christian people should move their governments to abstain from such policies and to provide a reasonable equality of economic opportunity."

"Christian influence," it is noted, "cannot be made effective without adequate factual knowledge. To meet this initial need, Christians should take measures to obtain information on world conditions more adequate and reliable than that now furnished by secular and nationalistic agencies, which are too prone to ignore or belittle the needs of alien people, or to express those needs in terms of sacrifice to be made by nations other than their own. Once the need of change is apprehended, its accomplishment depends upon governmental action. This will require of statesmen and politicians a broader vision than now exists of the true welfare of their nation. The heads of states, under whatever form of government, are ultimately dependent upon the support of their people, who must make it clear that they are prepared to accept temporary sacrifices in order that a greater good may ultimately emerge.". . .

◇◇◇◇

From the nature of the reports and the unanimity with which they were adopted, I draw certain conclusions:

1. Christianity as exemplified by the church leadership represented at Oxford is still vital. The reports deal realistically and deeply with highly controversial problems. They were drafted by men differing in nationality, race, culture,

creed, social position, and political affiliation. It would have been utterly impossible to secure agreement had there not been some controlling common denominator. That common denominator was found to be present. It was a genuine belief in Christ's life and teachings as the guide to human conduct.

I can emphasize this point by reference to another conference. Immediately preceding the Oxford Conference, I had attended at Paris the biennial meeting of the International Studies Conference. The topic of study was "Peaceful Change," the same topic as that dealt with by that portion of the Oxford report from which I quoted above. The Paris Conference was made up of students and men experienced in public affairs drawn from substantially the same nations as were represented at Oxford and selected to represent the best contribution which each country could make to an unofficial, dispassionate, and scholarly study of the chosen problem. No attempt was made to arrive at any agreed report. It was, however, apparent from the discussions which took place that it would have been impossible to agree either as to the nature and scope of the problem itself or the proper approach to its solution. Certainly not more than a small fraction of the delegates would have been willing to subscribe to such a statement as that which emanated from Oxford.

Each of the differing national viewpoints represented at Paris was also represented at Oxford. Only a powerful influence could have obliterated those differences. That this obliteration occurred at Oxford is clear evidence that the Christianity of those present was more than a name—it was a vital force.

2. A second conclusion which I draw from Oxford is that the churches are peculiarly qualified to promote a solution of the kind of problems which today vex mankind. These problems are not, like mathematical problems, susceptible of

an abstract, static solution. They require a dynamic solution, involving transition from one condition of affairs to another. If there be agreement upon the ultimate goal, then the way of solution becomes revealed. In this regard the churches have a great opportunity. They represent an important cross section of all mankind which, in theory at least, has a single, permanent and all-embracing objective: that human affairs be so ordered that "Thy will be done, on earth as it is in heaven."

The ineffectiveness of political agencies derives largely from the concept of "corporate responsibility." For example, directors of companies cannot, as a matter of existing law, indulge in generosities or largesses except as they believe that the stockholders whom they represent will gain a material advantage therefrom in the form of enhanced company profits.

Whatever the proper view may be as to so-called "corporate responsibility," and as to this the Oxford Conference made no pronouncement, the fact is that this concept is deeply rooted. This is serious when problems are so vast as not to be solvable by those who feel that they owe a duty of allegiance to certain groups alone. But in the eyes of God, all men are equal and their welfare is of equal moment. This is distinctively the Christian approach, and it is only through an approach of such universality that there is any promise of a solution. This, I think, was made apparent by the Oxford reports. It was not that the Oxford Conference discovered any new and clever formulas for the quick solution of stubborn problems. But it went far in showing that problems which otherwise seem unsolvable become susceptible of solution if approached from the standpoint of the universal brotherhood of man.

I do not mean to suggest that organized Christianity is the only instrument through which our problems may be solved,

or, as a corollary, that it is futile to seek to eliminate wars and
social unrest and injustice until the whole world has first
become Christianized. There was no disposition at Oxford to
contend for such a proposition, or to deny the contribution
which other religions and philosophies and social agencies can
make toward a solution of our human problems. The Christian
churches are powerful for good in so far as they propagate
spiritual truths. It is the truths which are important, not the
name, and those truths often appear under alien guise. As
such they should be recognized and welcomed and co-operated
with. But the Christian churches are unique in their combined qualifications. Not only are they founded upon a concept of universality, but they have in fact attained this to a
degree permitting them to approach every problem with
understanding of the diverse underlying national and social
conditions.

3. If the Oxford Conference showed the unique potentialities of the Christian churches, it also exemplified the
restraints necessary to prevent the churches becoming en-
meshed in partisan politics. The Conference did not claim
for its reports the imprimatur of divine, or even ecclesiastical,
authority. The reports themselves were, in the main, limited
to analyzing problems to a point which made evident the
spiritual failures which caused them. There was no advocacy
of particular political solutions. This was sound, for specific
measures will almost always involve matters of close judgment
and of expediency and will seldom be such an embodiment of
Christ's teaching that the church can permit the two to be
equated. Christ, for example, told a certain rich young man to
give all he had to the poor. But this gives us no clue to how far
the state should go in taxing those who have for the benefit of
those who have not. Normally, the state should not attempt

this to such a degree as to impair the functioning of the economic mechanism and thereby increase the net amount of need. But at this point we are involved in economics, not religion, and, as said in the Oxford Conference report on the Church and the Economic Order, "every tendency to identify the Kingdom of God with a particular structure of society or economic mechanism must result in moral confusion for those who maintain the system and a disillusionment for those who suffer from its limitations." This, however, does not mean that the church and state live in separate compartments. There must be communication. Normally this will be through the churches' so impressing spiritually upon the individual that his secular life will be affected thereby. It is notably in this respect that the churches have failed, and their first task is to make good this failure. Secondarily, and under special circumstance, the churches can accelerate and orient the reaction of the spiritual upon the secular by analyzing human problems so that the individual can more readily apply a spiritual test to political measures. But this must be attempted with caution. The Oxford Conference was so constituted as to make such an attempt permissible. There was present a wealth of knowledge and experience drawn from every nation, race, and social order. This was made available and utilized in a spirit of profound consecration. Such a combination of secular knowledge and spiritual consecration is indispensable if the churches are to attempt even an analysis of political and economic problems. Too often spiritual and secular motives become unconsciously mixed, and it requires unusual practical experience to detect the pitfalls which the worldly constantly prepare to secure for themselves the appearance of church benediction.

4. I have already referred to the extent to which the differences represented at the Conference were submerged by a

vital common denominator. This occurrence was indicative not merely of vitality, but it also demonstrated an amazing unity of thought and interpretation on the part of the different Christian denominations. There persisted, of course, the well-recognized differences of approach and emphasis which flowed from different ecclesiastical views and different conceptions of worship. No attempt was made to deal with or to eradicate such differences. Indeed, I think the generally prevalent view was that such differences were healthy and useful to preserve. Men worship God in different ways and interpret revelation in terms that vary according to education, race, and culture. But there emerged a unity in defense against pagan beliefs and a unity in offense against the problems which, if left unsolved, will inevitably destroy the Christian churches and prove that their name is a misnomer. . . .

◇◇◇◇

I had prepared for the Oxford Conference a paper entitled "The Problem of Peace in a Dynamic World." In concluding that paper I said that the major obstacles were created by pride and selfishness and that these could be got rid of "only by replacing them by some sentiment more dominant and gripping and which would contain in it the elements of universality as against particularity." I asked: "What of the democratic nations? What of the so-called Christian nations? They boast of high ideals, but have they the spiritual fire with which to drive out the petty instincts which bind them to a system which spells their doom?"

Since having attended the Oxford Conference, I think it possible that this question can be answered in the affirmative. It requires, however, that the spirit of Oxford should not die down but be projected through the membership — particularly the lay membership — of all our churches.

3

The Churches and World Order

Y ou are going out into the world at one of the critical
periods of human history. It will be the period when victory is consummated and when the task of preserving civilization will pass from the military to the civilian. The decade
following this war will determine whether the nations will
move toward another great war, or whether they will move
toward peaceful solutions of the future differences which inevitably will arise.

During this critical period, you will often ask yourselves,
and you will often be asked, What can the churches do to
influence the pattern of the future?

My judgment is that their influence can be decisive.

That judgment is very different from that with which I
started a career of international activity. For many years it
never occurred to me that the Christian gospel had any
practical bearing on the solution of international problems. I
came to my present view only after thirty years of experience
with futility.

At the Second Hague Peace Conference in 1907, I saw the

Address delivered to the graduating class of Princeton Theological Seminary
on May 16, 1944, published in *Theology Today*, October, 1944.

delegates of each nation, in the name of peace and humanity, maneuver for rules of war that would give their nation some advantage in the next war.

In Central America, I saw differences settled by the coercive use of our economic power.

At the Paris Peace Conference, I saw national rivalries so disunite the principal Allies that neither Wilson's program for a League of Nations, nor Clemenceau's program for a permanently weakened Germany, ever emerged from treaty words into living realities.

In 1923, during the French occupation of the Ruhr, I saw balance of power politics wreck a program substantially worked out between the German, French, and Belgian Governments whereby Germany would voluntarily cease passive resistance and resume reparation deliveries.

As counsel in relation to many postwar stabilization and rehabilitation loans, I saw their purpose frustrated. Borrowers used the proceeds to build up military establishments and lenders demanded the letter of their bond, while their nations refused to accept the goods and services through which alone repayment could be made.

At the German debt conferences which immediately followed Hitler's becoming chancellor, I saw Germany's policy poised between pursuit of international trade and pursuit of autarchy. I saw that policy swing to autarchy when the United States, for reasons of domestic policy, wrecked the contemporaneous London Economic Conference of 1933. Subsequently, in Germany, I saw the Nazi Party, by new scientific techniques for arousing mass emotion, instill in the German people a perverse belief in a "new order" to be achieved by force and administered by a German *Herrenvolk*.

At the 1937 Paris session of the Institute of Intellectual

Co-operation, held under the auspices of the League of Nations, I saw the impossibility of bringing the delegates present even to discuss the agreed topic of "peaceful change," lest it might be inferred that their own nation admitted the possibility of change to its disadvantage.

In China and Japan in 1938, I saw a Japanese military clique, which controlled the emperor, bend the Japanese people to their will by teaching that wherever the divine emperor led, there the people must fanatically follow.

In all of these matters, in which I played some part, I earnestly sought to promote peace and decent national relationships. Yet when a new and greater world war became certain, I saw that my record was one of complete futility. That personal failure was, of course, unimportant to anyone but myself. What was important was that I was not an isolated case. All of the good intentions of public officials and of private groups had been useless. So I took time out to analyze the record and to seek the cause of failure.

In that effort I obtained great enlightenment from one international event that, to me, stands out above all the others. That was the 1937 Oxford Conference on Church and State. It was made up of men and women who, like those who gathered at Pentecost, came "from every nation under heaven." There was but one bond of unity — that was faith in God as revealed by Jesus Christ. As at Pentecost, that bond of unity enabled us to understand each other. We discussed matters which, before, I had seen always give rise to violent dispute. We found intelligent, practical agreement as to how such matters should be dealt with. We did not find any formulas of quick and easy solution. But we did find that the toughest problems could be tackled in ways which, instead of creating discord, drew men together in fellowship.

How did that come about? What was the explanation of the amazing contrast between discussions which occurred in a Christian atmosphere and those which occurred in the conventional atmosphere of diplomacy?

When I analyzed the failures which I could judge of my personal knowledge, I found the causes.

There was idolatry. The national representatives who conducted foreign relations did more than seek the long-range welfare of their people. That would have been their duty. But they often personified their state as quasi-god. To enhance its power and prestige became their great objective. To that they subordinated the true welfare of the human beings who composed the nation.

There was hypocrisy. Each national representative usually considered that his own national group was predominantly endowed with virtue and all others with vice.

There was blindness. Men seldom saw beyond what served their nation's short-range material interest. With so limited a vision, the full elements of the problem were not grasped.

There was much evil emotion. Men readily became suspicious and resentful and angry. They had frequent rushes of blood to the head, which prevented their minds from working as keen tools to dissect the problem and resourcefully find ways for its solution.

There was little good emotion. Few were inspired to combat evil and to promote righteousness. They saw their tasks as isolated events in a materialistic world rather than as elements in some great progression toward human betterment. They were ineffective because they lacked the faith that is requisite for great deeds.

These causes of failure, I saw, were precisely those that Christ had sought to eradicate. He did not attempt to give

ready-made solutions of the problems of world order and
of social welfare. What he did was to tell men what were
the qualities they needed to solve those probems for themselves.

He told men to give their spiritual allegiance only to God
and to look upon human beings, rather than some personified
state, as the highest earthly unit of value.

He inveighed against hypocrisy and taught men to concern
themselves first with the evil in themselves.

He wanted men to see — to see far and to see truly. Blind
men, following blind leaders, he pointed out, will always end
up together in the pit.

He taught men to avoid the evil emotions of hatred and
blind vengefulness which so drive them to wreak destruction
that they cannot plan intelligently for construction.

He showed men a great vision and sought to implant in
them a sense of great purpose in life. He taught not a purely
contemplative religion but a dynamic faith which would make
men strong and powerful in action.

Now, of course, it was nothing new to me that Christ had
taught these things. I had learned that as a boy. What was
new was the realization that the qualities Christ taught were
the qualities that men needed in order to deal realistically
with practical problems. That lesson seems to me of the utmost
importance, and that is my excuse for telling you of it in the
way which may be the most graphic—namely, in terms of my
own experience. That lesson suggests, I think, the way in
which the churches and Christian ministers like yourselves
can decisively aid the cause of world order.

Some of you may have sufficient technical knowledge to
enable you to espouse concrete solutions of specific problems.
If you have that knowledge, it is of course your duty to put

it to work, for you are not only ministers of the gospel but citizens of your nation. But by and large, your greatest contribution will be to implant the qualities of soul and mind that Christ taught and then to get those qualities into actual use. It may be that you will have personal contact with those who implement national policy. You will find that such persons, even though avowed Christians, seldom use the Christian qualities I have referred to. That is the kind of omission which, if opportunity offers, you must seek to correct. Whether or not you have personal contact with public leaders, you will surely have contact with those who, as citizens, basically determine our national policies and choose our political leadership. The voters of this nation need to realize that leadership can safely be entrusted only to those who possess and will exercise, not only in word but in competent deed, the qualities taught by the great religions. Democracies always face great peril because the evil qualities I have mentioned seem, peculiarly, to have a mass appeal. Human beings in the mass find it pleasant to deify their corporate group; they like to be told that they are pre-eminently endowed with virtues; they get a pleasurable thrill by being stirred to passionate hate; and they often choose for themselves political leaders who pander to those trends. That happened, to an extreme degree, in Germany. There Hitler came to power through the constitutional processes of democracy. The German churches had failed to make the people Christian in the sense that, as citizens, they would reject leadership which exemplified qualities which Christ most strongly condemned. That same sort of thing happens to a degree everywhere. So, I say, your greatest contribution toward world order will be to bring Christian citizens to realize that their political leadership will be futile and end only in disaster unless it is the leader-

ship of men who have and will use qualities of the kind
Christ taught. . . . .

◇◇◇◇

I think the vision Christ taught was total vision, which sees
all the facts. Like Pilgrim, we must move forward through
obstacles; we do not soar above them. Unless we see those
obstacles, we shall stumble and get nowhere.

One reality we need to see is that the society of nations is
in a most primitive stage of development. We have, in essence,
a society of some sixty members who have never even established a common meeting place. There is little community
sentiment. Each member goes his own way, and power,
whether or not actually used, primarily determines whether
one or another nation gets what it wants or keeps what it
wants. As Lord Lothian constantly emphasized, the society of
nations is in a state of anarchy.

No society moves at a single bound from the primitive stage
of anarchy to a highly developed order. That comes through
gradual stages.

The first stage is psychological. There must be an intellectual and emotional conviction that the existing system is so
bad that it must be changed, even though that means, for
some, forgoing advantages that they have the power to grasp.
It takes hard and cruel experience to get a primitive group
into that frame of mind. Those who think they have the
power, or can get the power, to do what they want, usually
prefer a power system.

Two world wars may have brought the nations really to
want to organize their society so that principles, rather than
relative power, settle conflicts of desire. However, we must not
take that for granted. Such a sentiment is the usual accompani-
ment of a hard war. But when victory comes, nations which

emerge with great power, or which want to develop power in order to reverse the verdict of a lost war, are apt to conclude that, after all, a power system is the best.

If that happens after this war, we will again fail to have the state of mind which must precede any genuine progress toward world order. To prevent that psychological relapse must be the concern of those, like yourselves, who aspire to moral leadership. . . .

◇◇◇◇

I am told nowadays that there is much discouragement among our people. That is largely due to increasing realization that permanent peace cannot be easily and quickly assured by military victory or by some treaty formula. That cause of discouragement is to me a most encouraging fact. All great wars give rise to visionary hopes that victory itself will assure lasting peace. Usually the treaty of victory has proclaimed permanent peace, and that has satisfied the popular demand. Men have not seen how superficial that was until a new war was actually in the making. Now we know, in time, that to win a victory and to proclaim a peace does not suffice. To know that is the beginning of wisdom.

To achieve world order is a long, hard task. It will only have begun when the fighting stops. It is not a task for those who are weary or of faint heart. It calls for men who are clear of vision, strong of faith, and competent in deed. Fortunately, there is a goodly number of those men among our leaders and among the rank and file of our people. How much they can achieve, and how quickly, depends on whether their ranks are steadily augmented. We need many more who possess and will use the qualities Christ taught. To assure that is your task.

4

A Diplomat and His Faith

IN SEPTEMBER, 1951, the President asked me to undertake the diplomatic negotiation of a Japanese peace treaty. I was given broad discretionary authority, subject only to certain security requirements stipulated for by the Department of Defense. The responsibility was a heavy one. There was urgent need for action, for already the occupation was ending its fifth year and further inaction would breed disastrous bitterness and resentment against us in Japan. On the other hand, there were some fifty Allied nations which had declared war against Japan, and they differed much among themselves. It had been possible to achieve unity for war against Japan, but how could we achieve unity for peace with Japan?

As I pondered the problem, my thoughts went back ten years to the time when the Federal Council of Churches had organized its Commission on a Just and Durable Peace and I had become chairman of that Commission. I recalled the Statement of Guiding Principles, which had been adopted at Delaware, Ohio, in 1942, with its triumphant proclamation of the supremacy of moral law and of the special responsibility

First in a series of articles on "How My Faith Helped in a Decisive Hour," *The Christian Century,* March 19, 1952.

which devolved upon the United States to bring international relations into conformity with that moral law. Such pronouncements are often made in religious circles by those who have no actual responsibility for the conduct of affairs. But would it be prudent and possible, now that I had a national responsibility, actually to practice what we had preached?

As I reviewed the international scene, I saw powerful influences which seemed not to accord with the moral law of which we had spoken.

In the countries which had been invaded by Japan, such as the Philippines, Indo-China, and Indonesia, there was much hatred and vengefulness. In this country we had not forgotten Pearl Harbor, Bataan, and the "March of Death." In countries not actually invaded but threatened with invasion, such as Australia and New Zealand, there was widespread fear and a desire that the treaty should seek to make Japan permanently weak and unarmed. Among those who had experienced prewar commercial competition from Japan, there was a widespread desire for a treaty which would cripple Japan commercially so that in shipbuilding, ship operations, textiles, fishing, and so on, she could never again be a serious competitor. In Asian countries, peoples who hated and feared Western colonialism wanted a treaty which would totally eradicate Western influence from Japan. Some, who saw the international problem as primarily a military one, wanted to make Japan into a great military bastion against Soviet Russia. Others wanted a treaty which would compel Japan, by discriminatory provisions, to become the proving ground for an experiment in disarmament which their own countries rejected.

These were the sentiments that were most vocal, and at first glance it seemed that the peace would have to draw on some such sentiments for its support. However, I was not hopeful that it would be possible in this way to get a just and durable peace. It might perhaps be possible to get a piece of paper labeled "Peace." But as one who had had close contact with the making, and then the unmaking, of the Treaty of Versailles, I realized how undependable was a peace treaty that was discriminatory, that had to be forcibly imposed, and that gave expression to the evil passions which war leaves as its aftermath. Such a treaty almost inevitably creates a new series of evil passions and thus perpetuates a cycle of recurrent war.

It seemed to me that here, if ever, was the occasion to try to make a peace which would invoke the principles of the moral law. The opportunity was the greater because General MacArthur was prepared to put all of his great prestige behind the invoking of a new concept in international relations. So we drafted a treaty which invoked the spirit of forgiveness to overcome the spirit of vengefulness; the spirit of magnanimity to overcome the spirit of hatred; the spirit of humanity and fair play to overcome the spirit of competitive greed; the spirit of fellowship to overcome the spirit of arrogance and discrimination; and the spirit of trust to overcome the spirit of fear.

The territorial terms of peace had already been determined at Potsdam over five years before and had actually been put into effect through the elimination of Japanese jurisdiction over Korea, Formosa, South Sakhalin, and the Kurile, Ryukyu, and Bonin Islands. To the extent that those decisions were debatable on their merits, we planned to keep open the possibility of future adjustments.

As far as reparations were concerned, the principle of reparations would be affirmed, as a matter of simple justice. However, justice would be tempered with mercy by provisions which would assure that reparations could not be exacted which would impair Japan's viable economy or would throw foreign-exchange burdens upon Japan. In substance, reparations would be in terms of the creditor nations' availing of the assets which Japan had in surplus, namely, a surplus trained population and surplus industrial facilities. These could be put to use for account of the reparation creditors, provided they supplied the raw materials. Thus the arrangement would not be a burden upon Japan's ability to buy abroad the goods and raw materials that she needs to maintain a decent standard of living.

Subject to these provisions, the treaty would restore Japan to complete and equal fellowship in the community of free nations. Japan would not be subjected to commercial or political discriminations which, however well intentioned, the Allied powers were unwilling to accept for themselves. As to armament, that would be left to Japan's own decision. The treaty would not compel armament, nor would it require disarmament. The ugly past would be merged into an act of reconciliation by a treaty which placed trust in the desire of the Japanese people themselves to become self-respecting and honored members of the world community.

We contemplated also procedures which would be those of reconciliation. I recalled vividly how, at the end of World War I, the German peace delegation was put into a barbed-wire enclosure at Versailles, exposed to the populace as animals in a zoo and denied any personal contact with Allied delegates. That procedure in itself had gone far to ensure that the peace treaty, even though it had been meritorious in substance, would be deeply resented.

We proposed in this case to consult fully with the Japanese, who by their loyal compliance with the surrender terms had won the right to be fully heard. Indeed, after the basic prin-

ciples had been discussed with the principally concerned
Allied powers, the Japanese were the first to be consulted with
respect to the detailed application of these principles.

The success of the program which I have sketched depended
upon there being within the Allied countries, including the
United States, a majority who both believed in moral principles and were willing to make their beliefs effectively felt
as a political force. We went about the world trying to find out
whether that was the case. Greatly to our satisfaction, and I
must admit somewhat to our surprise, we found that when
the issues were clearly presented, there was little doubt as to
where the balance of power lay. It lay in favor of the principles
of the moral law. Even in countries where there was under-
standably great bitterness and great fear, the majority were for
reconciliation and for trust.

After a year of negotiation, a period which seemed long at
the time but which was short considering the complexities of
the task, there assembled at San Francisco the delegates of
fifty-two nations. Of these, three were from the Soviet Communist bloc and came with the announced intention of
attempting to block the treaty. The other forty-nine, constituting all but two of the fifty-one non-Communist countries
which had been invited, came to sign the treaty and to express
their nations' support in words which showed, unmistakably
and eloquently, the tremendous appeal of the moral principles which the draft treaty had invoked.

The prime minister of Japan, speaking from a platform
where the flag of Japan would soon stand with the flags of the
Allied countries, said: "It is not a treaty of vengeance, but an
instrument of reconciliation. The Japanese delegation gladly
accepts this fair and generous treaty." And the chairman of
the conference, Dean Acheson, concluded it with a bene-

diction never before pronounced at such a gathering but which had been made appropriate by all that had gone before: "I close this conference with words which in many languages, in many forms, in many religions, have brought comfort and strength: 'May the peace of God, which passeth all understanding, be amongst us and remain with us always.' "

In a paper which I wrote in 1942 for the Federal Council's Commission on a Just and Durable Peace, I said that communism had moved into a spiritual vacuum which had resulted from the loss elsewhere of a dynamic faith. At San Francisco there was no spiritual vacuum. The atmosphere was charged with the power of the moral law, and those who denied moral law were ignominiously put to rout.

I do not exaggerate the importance of that moment. It does not mean that we made a perfect treaty. Indeed, the delegates constantly disclaimed perfection. It does not mean that the peace will necessarily be durable. That will depend upon the future. The treaty, while it did not express hatred, jealousy, or vengefulness, did not and could not obliterate these sentiments from the world. They persist and might again take control and, through irresponsible national action, inflict the discriminations which the treaty itself rejected. Evil ambition might be reborn in Japan.

On the other hand, if we do not exaggerate, also we need not belittle. What was done showed that moral principles are not something to be relegated to Sunday services in our churches. They can be brought boldly and unashamedly into the arena of world affairs. There *is* a moral law which, no less than physical law, undergirds our world. It *is* relevant to the corporate life of men and the ordering of human society. It *can* be drawn upon — indeed, it *must* be drawn upon — if mankind is to escape chaos and recurrent war.

5

Patriotism and the American Tradition

IT IS indeed a great privilege for me to be here and to have the opportunity of talking with you on an occasion which for me is full of sentiment. It was just one hundred years ago that my grandfather, John W. Foster, was graduated from this university. It was just fifty years ago that he received from this university the honorary degree which, I understand, the university plans to confer upon me tomorrow. My grandfather, whose name I bear, exerted a great influence over my life, and he had ideals and purposes which I have tried to make my own.

He was a deeply patriotic American. He belonged to the period which saw this country rapidly developing from a small Atlantic Coast group into a nation that spread across the continent. He fought to preserve the Union; and then, on diplomatic missions and as Secretary of State, he helped to spread the influence of this nation throughout the world both in Europe and in Asia.

He deeply revered his forebears, who had been pioneers in settling this part of our nation. He wrote a private booklet inscribed "Don't Let the Little Ones Forget," in which he

Baccalaureate address at Indiana University, June 12, 1955.

told for his descendants the story of his own forebears: his grandfather (my great-great-grandfather) on whose grave I laid a wreath today, and his father.

To me that story has symbolized the spirit of our nation. I vividly recall being told of how my great-grandfather, as a young boy of seventeen, had struck out into the West to get away from what seemed to him the overpopulated East. After a foot voyage of exploration, he had fixed upon a forest tract in southern Indiana as a future homestead. He then brought his aged parents — his father was then seventy-nine years old — from the East to settle here and gained a livelihood by hunting and by cutting hickory for hogshead hoops and floating them on a raft down the Ohio and Mississippi Rivers to New Orleans, where hogsheads were needed for molasses. Then he would walk back through the twelve hundred miles of dangerous trails from New Orleans to his log-cabin home here in Indiana. Finally he become a farmer, a merchant, and then a judge in the growing community he had helped to create.

That spirit of enterprise, that vision, that industry, and that rugged independence have been characteristic of our nation. There are indeed few Americans who cannot find in their family history similar stories of those who risked much and endured much to bring a dream into reality. It is those qualities which, within the short span of one hundred and fifty years, have brought our people from national infancy into forming the greatest nation on earth.

In some quarters there has developed a tendency to scorn patriotism. Indeed, there are a few who find patriotism unfashionable and who go so far as to assume that institutions and ideas are better if only they bear a foreign label. Also there is a theory that this mood is necessary if we are to develop international institutions and maintain international peace.

It seems to me that love of country is one of the great and indispensable virtues. No community is weaker because the members of the families which make it up — the mother, the father, the sons, the daughters, the brothers and sisters — are bound together by distinctive ties of love, respect, and admiration. So I am convinced that the family of nations will not be the poorer or the more fragile because the peoples who form the different nations have a special affection and pride for their own people and for the nation they form.

I recall that St. Paul took great pride, which he did not attempt to conceal, in the achievements of his own people. To me, one of the most inspiring chapters in the Bible is the eleventh chapter of Hebrews, where St. Paul recalls, in epic words, the great deeds which had been wrought through faith by national heroes, men and women.

Recently I was asked to open an exhibit of the oldest-known print of the Bible, in the Aramaic language, and in that connection to select one of my favorite verses. I selected that portion of The Epistle to the Hebrews where St. Paul, after the historical recital to which I allude, concludes by saying, "Seeing that we are compassed about by so great a cloud of witnesses, let us run with endurance the race that is set before us."

If it was appropriate for St. Paul to entertain those sentiments, I think it is equally appropriate for us. We too of our nation can look back with pride to the great figures which our nation has produced, who through faith wrought much.

Surely we too can feel "that we are compassed about by a great cloud of witnesses" who are observing our conduct and who by their spirit seek to inspire us to carry forward the great national and international tasks to which they dedicated their lives and to which they committed our nation by their strivings and by their faith.

Our national course has to a unique degree been shaped by religious beliefs. Our people have in the main been God-fearing people. They believed in moral principles derived from a Source above us. They were dedicated to human liberty because they believed that men had been endowed by their Creator with inalienable rights. So they provided that those rights must at all times be respected, assuring the sovereignty of the individual against the dictatorship of the state. They were confident that the human liberty they thus assured would not be exercised recklessly and in disregard of fellow men, because they were confident that our citizens would obey the moral law which prescribes the Ten Commandments of the Old Testament and the two great commandments of the New Testament, "Thou shalt love thy neighbor as thyself" and "Whatsoever ye would that men should do to you, do ye even so to them."

As George Washington pointed out in his Farewell Address, religion and morality are the two indispensable supports of a free society. "In vain," he said, "would that man claim the tribute of patriotism who should labor to subvert these great pillars of human happiness, these firmest props of the duties of men and citizens." Indeed, a society which is not religious cannot tolerate much freedom. It is dangerous to give freedom to those who do not feel under moral compulsion to exercise self-control and who are unwilling to make sacrifices for the good of others.

It results that true patriotism, which vitalizes liberty and freedom for ourselves, can never be a purely selfish force. That has been ever evident so far as our nation was concerned. Our people have always been endowed with a sense of mission in the world. They have believed that it was their duty to help men everywhere to get the opportunity to be and to do what God designed. They saw a great prospect and were filled with a great purpose. As said in the opening paragraph of *The Federalist* papers, "It seems to have been reserved to the people of this country, by their conduct and example, to decide whether societies of men are capable of establishing good government." "Failure on their part," it continues, would be "the general misfortune of mankind."

Under the impulsion of that faith there developed here an area of spiritual, intellectual, and economic vigor the like of which the world had never seen. It was no exclusive preserve; indeed, sharing was the central theme. Millions were welcomed here from other lands, all to share equally the opportunities of the founders and their heirs. Through missionary activities and the establishment of schools and colleges abroad, American ideals were carried throughout the world. Our Government gave aid and comfort to those elsewhere who sought to increase human freedom.

These have been the characteristics of our nation since its foundation, and those characteristics have persisted. They today make our nation the leader in the struggle to maintain liberty in the world. I believe we can say that in these times, when despotism menaces as never before, our nation is playing a part worthy of our forebears and is imbued with the spirit of those who founded our republic. We have availed of every opportunity, whether it be through the United Nations or through mutual security associations with other free nations, to make our influence felt in support of freedom. We have, as a matter of enlightened self-interest, contributed largely out of our vast productivity to others who, if left alone, could not sustain the freedom and independence for which they yearn.

All of that is in the American tradition. We can be happy that that tradition thrives and is vigorous, and we can take pride in the fact that, inspired by our founders who saw a great vision, we are indeed with steadfastness pursuing the course upon which they embarked us.

There come times in the life of peoples when their work of creation ends. It is easy to diagnose the symptoms of that national decadence. It is seen when a people lose their sense of mission in the world, when they think only of themselves, when they forget the Biblical injunction that, although we have different offices, we are all members one of another and that those who are strong ought to bear the infirmities of the weak. No one, be he individual or nation, is truly great who does not have the will and the capacity to help others or who is without a sense of mission.

We can take pride in our nation because since the day of its creation, and with but few lapses, our purposes have been large and their goals have been humane. We can rejoice that that spirit animates our nation today and makes us still young, still vital, and still capable of great endeavor. Our youth, such as you who now enter into the larger world, are spirited, not selfish nor fearful. Our religious heritage and our national traditions are not forgotten. As we are faithful to their guidance, we can have the satisfaction which comes to those who, in fellowship, are embarked on the great adventure of building peacefully a nation and a world of human liberty and justice.

II

The American Heritage

John Foster Dulles was not only a convinced Christian. He was a loyal American, proud of his nation's history and traditions, persuaded that an intelligent understanding of that heritage was essential equipment for citizens who would serve their country effectively.

But he believed profoundly that "something has gone wrong with our nation," that what was wrong was a loss of vision and of courage, that what was required was the recovery of "a righteous and dynamic faith."

This is the burden of the writings and speeches that follow. They were prepared for the most diverse publics, from the readers of Life magazine to the graduating class at the National War College.

It was a steadily deepening emphasis with him. It was anticipated in his first book, War, Peace and Change, written in 1938; but there it holds a subordinate place. That book speaks of "the decline of religion as a vital influence" (p. 115). In the successor volume, however, War or Peace, published in 1950, the penultimate chapter, which immediately precedes a summarizing "Conclusion," is devoted to "Our Spiritual Need," where both his disquiet over the loss of national vision and his own prescription for remedy are set forth in the bluntest and most forceful terms.

6

A Righteous Faith

A LL GREAT wars bring with them some sort of spiritual revival. For when we are at war material things must be sacrificed. Money, goods, life itself, are poured into the fiery furnace. Men then grope for spiritual things as the only available alternative.

Too often, however, the spiritual revival of war is but shallow emotionalism. Men fill their souls with hatred and vengefulness and they deify their nation. When the war is over, these passions quickly subside and materialism again becomes rampant.

If this occurs in the United States it will be a serious matter, for already before this war our great weakness was lack of that faith that makes men strong. If we now merely win military victory, that will not make us safe unless we also win back faith such as sustained us when we were yet small and materially weak.

If we look back over the last two hundred years, that will make plain what I mean. Until the time of the First World War three peoples held undisputed leadership in the world. These three were the British, the French, and ourselves. We three were not great because of our numbers, for no one of us constituted 10 per cent of the world's population. We were not great because of our natural wealth, for Great Britain and France are poor countries and, during most of this period, the resources of the United States were undeveloped. We were great because our three peoples were imbued with and radiated great faiths. These were not perfect faiths, but they incorporated the Christian idea that man owes a duty to fellow man. We sought our own advantage, but we sought it in ways that would also advantage others. Our spirit was one of mission in the world. Often we were hypocrites, but even that showed that we felt under a moral compulsion to justify what we did as being for the welfare of others.

The French toward the end of the eighteenth century had exploded upon a world of despotism the revolutionary slogan of human "Liberty, Equality, and Fraternity." Their belief in the rights of the individual partook of a religious fervor, and so contagious was their faith that it changed the face of the Western world and broke the political chains that were fastened upon the people.

In England, inventive genius showed how man's labor could be made infinitely more productive by using mechanical power and machinery. Thereby raw materials could quickly and cheaply be turned into finished goods and standards of living greatly raised. The possibilities thus opened up were carried by England into the uttermost parts of the earth and were given moral sanction as a carrying of the "white man's burden." Today we laugh at that phrase, but under its influence hundreds of thousands of Britain's best youth went forth to do what they believed to be in the general welfare. Britain gained, but in the process more was done to improve the general lot of mankind than ever before in any comparable period of time.

◇◇

We in the United States became conscious of a "manifest destiny" and "American dream." We visioned here a vast continent to be opened up to the repressed and oppressed of other lands. We saw that we might fashion here a state of ordered freedom that would be a beacon in the world. We went far toward making that dream come true. Millions came to us from other lands and found here the material opportunities and the spiritual freedoms which they had vainly sought for themselves and their children.

All that we did, at home or abroad, was profoundly influenced by our Christian faith. As Dean Weigle shows us, our domestic political evolution was determined by men's conception of their duty as sons of God. And abroad, wherever trading posts sprang up, there, too, a mission post was planted.

Thus each of our three peoples had hold of something bigger than ourselves, something that forced us into a kind of partnership sharing with the rest of the world. It was that that made us great and strong. It was that that made us safe and free.

The beginning of this century showed a steady exhaustion of our spiritual springs. Woodrow Wilson, it is true, inspired a wartime idealism that did much to bring us victory. But that was a flare-up that quickly subsided. We emerged from that war — the French, the British, and ourselves — as burnt-out peoples. We no longer felt a sense of mission in the world. We had nothing so big that it had to be shared. Indeed, we had so lost faith in our own institutions that we felt it necessary to shelter them from contact with the outer world. We sought only to be left alone, and in our isolated and, as we thought, "matured" economies, we found little to do except to squabble over the partition of the material wealth we had theretofore created. Upon the world there descended a spirit of disillusionment and discouragement. The youth were without opportunity or hope, the workers were without employment, and the aged were without security. All were without faith. Even in church circles where the word "faith" was still used, it had lost any real significance.

It is impossible to perpetuate a spiritual vacuum. So, inevitably, it came about that here and there, throughout the world, new faiths were born. In Russia, out of the collapse of 1917, there had arisen a militant faith in Marxian communism. Like all great faiths, it could not be confined. It sought world-wide realization through world revolution. Next Italy seemed, momentarily, to recapture the tradition that was Rome's, and, under that pagan impulse, sought glory in Africa. In Germany arose a militant faith in a "new order" under which the national barriers of Europe would be torn down and each non-German given an allotted task to be performed under the dominance of a German *Herrenvolk*. Japan had meanwhile come under the control of a military clique who fanatically sought a "co-prosperity sphere," which would give Japan in the Orient that which Germany sought in the Western world.

These faiths were largely repugnant to us. In the case of Germany, Italy, and Japan they were evil faiths that led to war — and will lead to frustration — because they asserted racial supremacy and exalted force and violence as the means of achieving it. But, good or bad, they were faiths that, while they lasted, made men strong. We have been startled by what those nations have performed. We were stupefied when Germany, enfeebled, disarmed, and dismembered by the Treaty of Versailles, grew into a blazing volcano that erupted over all Europe. We were aghast when Japan in a few months took under her military sway the vast areas of the Indies, Malaya, and Burma. We were wholly taken by surprise by the valor and tenacity of Russia's resistance and forced to a total revaluation of things Russian.

If history teaches anything, it is that no nation is great and no nation is strong unless its people are imbued with a faith. It also shows that no nation can be *permanently* great or *permanently* strong unless that faith be a *righteous* faith that is compatible with the welfare and the dignity of others. Unless during this war we regain that kind of faith, then military victory will serve no permanent good. For again new faiths will arise to attack us and in the long run we will succumb. The impact of the dynamic upon the static — while it may be resisted in detail — will ultimately destroy that which it attacks. The First World War, this World War, and the next world war may go down in history as a series of rear-guard actions by disillusioned peoples who, equipped only with the material products of past greatness, sought valiantly but vainly to resist the penetration of alien faiths.

The Protestant churches of America are awake to the spiritual need that faces our nation. They are determined to do all that lies in their power to assure that out of this war will be born, not just ephemeral passions, but a faith that will endure and that will project us into the world as a great force for righteousness. As Professor Hocking puts it, the church must seek "to discern 'the mind of Christ' and to announce concretely the divine attitude which man in wartime may strive toward." . . .

◇◇◇◇

We know that if the principles we have proclaimed become mandatory in the consciousness of American people, they will know in what direction to move and they will move in that direction and they will thereby assure that our nation will again become a dynamic moral force in the world.

What is the great obstacle we encounter? It is not opposition to our ends. Almost everybody would agree that it would be a nice thing if the American people were again united and enthused by a great dynamic faith. The difficulty we encounter is that men are skeptical of the way we propose to get that faith. Christ said, "I am the way." But most people have ceased to believe it. They have come to look upon Jesus as an impractical idealist, and they consider that those of us who urge men to follow his way are uttering a counsel of perfection that is unrelated to the practical needs of the times. For that attitude the church leaders of the past have a heavy responsibility. They have often made Christ seem to be wholly different from what he really was. Some have made it appear that Christ taught an "idealism" that was wholly unrelated to worldly problems and that served men only when they died. Others, going to the opposite extreme, have sought to put Christ's authority behind specifics that practical men could see were of dubious worth. The truth is that Christ was neither impractical nor was he specific. He told men, not *what* to do, but how to acquire the qualities of soul and of mind that would enable *them* to know what to do.

I recall that Christ ministered at a time when international and social problems existed in aggravated form. Much of the world was under the heel of a military dictator and labor was largely slavery. Tiberius had achieved for Rome what Hitler has sought for Germany. Yet Christ advocated no specific revolts and sponsored no specific reforms. This cannot be because he was indifferent to the human misery that surrounded him. Rather, he sought to do something bigger and more enduring than to cure the particular evils of his day. He sought to show men how, throughout the ages, they might find the

way to surmount evil that would constantly be reappearing in
ever-changing form. That way, he taught, was for men to act
out of visions that would see clear, minds that would think
straight, and hearts that would comprehend the essential unity
and equal worthiness of all human beings. He inveighed
against hatred and vengefulness, self-conceit and deification
of one's particular nation, race, or class. He did so not only
because such emotions are repugnant to God's will for man,
but also because they always make men incompetent to deal
with human problems. They create those blind masses and
those blind leaders who, he pointed out, end up together in
the pit.

Jesus was, as Dr. Fosdick tells us, "everlastingly right." "He
was the 'truth' — the realistic, factual revelation of what life
actually means." Until we believe that and act accordingly, we
are the ones who are impractical. Surely the catastrophes that
inevitably overtake those who operate on anti-Christian principles powerfully argue that it is those principles that are not
true.

What, then, shall we do to equip ourselves to deal with the
problem of our time? The answer is eternally the same: we
must develop those qualities of vision, of soul, and of mind
that Christ taught and then act under the directive of those
qualities. Let us glimpse at what that means.

If we have vision, what is it we shall see? We shall, like
Christ, see a multitude who hunger. That multitude is all
about us — some near, some afar. They hunger not only for
things material but for things spiritual. We would not be
seeing truly if we saw only material wants. Such needs exist
and they are great. But the greatest need is not for things.
Men hunger for sympathy and fellowship that will lift them

out of their physical environment. They crave the vibrant thrill that comes from creative effort. They need a religious faith that will carry them through tribulations which no material wealth can prevent.

Christ saw, and if we have vision we too will see, that material things serve chiefly as instruments for bringing into being those nonmaterial values that men need most. When he told the rich young man to give all to the poor, he saw not so much the material advantage for the poor as the value of the spiritual outlook that would prompt such an act. By similar standards he appraised the widow's gift of her mites and Mary's sacrifice of her precious ointment. So it is that as our eyes are opened we will see material needs, but we will see them in subordinate relationship to spiritual needs.

If we have hearts that are comprehending, we shall, like Christ, be moved with compassion. We shall hear the cry of the masses that a way be found to save them and their children from the death, the misery, the starvation of body and soul which recurrent war and economic disorder now wreak upon man. We shall be so moved by that cry that we shall resolutely dedicate ourselves to the achievement of a better order. We shall find, in that dedication, something that will make our own lives worth living and our own nation worth preserving.

If, in addition to acquiring vision and human understanding, we free our minds from warping emotions — like hate and prejudice — then we can think straight and approach with competence the technical problems of our time. The broad principles that should govern our international conduct are not obscure. . . . The overwhelming majority of Christians would surely agree with them. So, too, for that matter, would those of other great faiths. But that is not enough. We need men who, as citizens, will think out the application of those principles to the daily life of our nation. That is something that everyone must do for himself. The church cannot and should not try to do that for him. If the church follows Christ's example, it will proclaim eternal verities in terms such that their practical significance is made plain, but it will avoid sponsoring specifics that necessarily must be compromises compounded out of worldly knowledge. That is what the citizen must do, and he can do it competently if he equips himself with the qualities of vision, of soul, and of mind that Christ taught.

Finally, we must act. Christ did not teach a purely contemplative religion. "Let your light so shine before men, that they may see your good works." We must not be paralyzed by fear lest what we do may not be perfect. Neither must we wait until someone develops a spectacular plan for achieving at once all that we desire. Action is a thing that, itself, is good. It is out of action that there is born a sense of creative power and purpose. Every individual, every nation, must make an effort to find opportunities where faith can be converted into action. Those opportunities are always available. It is unimportant if initially our acts, as individuals or as a nation, are unspectacular. For if what we do is prompted by clear vision, human comprehension, and clear thinking, we will be surprised at the fruitful consequence of what we do. Inspired and urged on by those consequences, we will steadily move forward, enlarging the practical expression of our faith and developing for it a defined and expanding pattern. As our national faith is made manifest by works, and grows under that stimulus, its influence will be contagious throughout the world. As the evil faiths that combat us collapse, leaving death and ruin as their fruit, the faith that makes us strong will encompass the earth.

It will unite men, as never before, in common and constructive purpose.

I am full of hope. On every side there is evidence that a new faith is emerging and that this faith will be born out of the gospel of Jesus Christ. I am told that there is one book that cannot be kept in adequate supply at our Army camps. That book is the New Testament. Throughout the land, church meetings and study groups are seeing, with Christian vision, the opportunities that open before us. I believe that the spiritual rebirth we are witnessing will not be spurious, but that it will give us an abiding faith. That faith, now in its formative stage, we must constantly nurture, and we must constantly test it by the mind of Christ. Above all, we need to have it shared by the many millions who, at this Christmas time, celebrate the birth of our Lord, but who otherwise live their lives without regard for the fact that he *is* the way, the truth, and the life.

7

The American Vision

THIS meeting opens the churches' National Mission on World Order. By that mission we seek to revive in our people a sense of destiny in the performance of a great work of creation. Upon the success of our effort, with parallel efforts by others, depends the future of our nation. For we are at one of those critical periods that can readily mark the end of our greatness.

We have been a people of vision and self-confidence. Our founders, though a mere handful of colonists, from the start conceived of their task as of world-wide import. They saw a great prospect, and were filled with a great purpose. The opening paragraph of *The Federalist* papers reads: "It seems to have been reserved to the people of this country, by their conduct and example, to decide whether societies of men are capable of establishing good government." Failure on their part, it continues, would be "the general misfortune of mankind." Moreover, they did not see their experiment as something to be conducted under the conditions of a laboratory. That would have meant little to others than themselves. They

---

Address at the opening of the churches' National Mission on World Order, Cathedral of St. John the Divine, New York City, October 28, 1943.

had the courage to launch their principles into the world. The thirteen colonies did not form themselves into a closed political unit. They adopted a constitution which was an "open-end" instrument, designed to bring more areas and more people into federal union. By the operation of this provision the original states and their citizens quickly became a minority. They had disdained subtle formulas for perpetuating their own control, and fearlessly entrusted their destiny to the inherent soundness of the structure they had conceived.

Not only was their society designed boldly to expand into the world but it was designed to absorb from the rest of the world. Millions were welcomed here from other lands, to share equally the opportunities of the founders and their heirs.

Under the impulsion of that creative and courageous spirit, the original vision assumed reality. Within a few generations there existed here an area of spiritual, intellectual, and economic vigor the like of which the world had never seen. Americans had, I know, their share of human defects. But their dominant qualities were creative.

The best proof of that is the judgment of others. Throughout the nineteenth century the American accomplishment was everywhere recognized as outstanding, and no land is without institutions inspired by our example.

Another objective test of our achievement is the security we enjoyed. We had no army and only a small navy. We were the least militarized of any Western nation. Yet for a century we were not endangered. No foreign people sought to destroy the great American experiment which they admired and in the fruits of which they shared.

Then something happened. We lost our vision. We no longer conceived that we were creating for the benefit of mankind. We lost our courage. We doubted that we could any longer endow our society with the capacity to expand and to absorb. We closed, *de facto*, our political orbit. This was not because we had achieved a higher order of morality which judged the growth of federal union to be evil. It was because we were afraid. We dared not allow more resources and more people to come into equal sharing with us. "America for the Americans" became our slogan. To keep what we had became our basis for action. On all fronts we began to build barriers — higher tariffs, severe restraints on immigration, and increasing exclusion of foreign capital.

When we had to decide whether to join the League of Nations, we refused. Some good reasons could be found for that action. But the reason that was decisive was a bad reason: it was fear.

I know that there are always prophets of evil and that to them the past always seems glorious and the present pallid. But sometimes they are right. The fact of our fallen estate can be proved by the same objective tests that proved our greatness. Half of the population of the world — one billion people — will face tomorrow the task of rebuilding their economic, social, and political order. All their established institutions will have been swept away. Where will they turn for guidance, example, and inspiration? One hundred years ago, fifty years ago, they surely would have turned to us. But they will not do so as we are today, for we present the spectacle of a people who have lost confidence in themselves.

A further proof of our changed condition is to be found in the dangers from without we have had to meet. It is no mere accident that we have now had to fight two great wars in quick succession — wars to parry the first real menaces to our national life. We had become rich and materially powerful, but we were no longer a life-giving society. Daring nothing, we endangered all.

What has happened is grave. It means that our children and grandchildren will not breathe an air suffused with the elixir of creative effort. They will grow up in a sordid atmosphere of quarreling about the division of what former generations created. The shadow of danger will be upon them. It will be a danger that neither armament nor alliances can avert, for such externals never compensate for lack of spiritual power.

There comes a time in the life of every great people when its work of creation ends. Perhaps that hour has struck for us. But it need not be so. Essentially we are still vital and capable of great endeavor. Our youth are not soft or fearful of peril; they crave adventure. Our tradition and our heritage are not forgotten. No forces that we cannot master compel our national decadence. If, however, we are to avoid that fate and recapture the spirit that made us great, we must first diagnose and then cure the malady that attacks us. Something has happened. What is it that has happened and why?

We have had to meet the severest test that can come to a people, that is, the test of prosperity. We have failed to meet that test successfully.

It was said by Christ that material things would be added unto those who seek first the Kingdom of God and his righteousness. But when that happens, then comes the great trial. For, as Christ warned, those material things can readily become the rust that corrodes men's souls.

Thus there often occurs a typical cycle. Men who feel a sense of duty to some higher Being strive here to do his will. Because of their faith, they have power and virtue and simple wisdom. They build not only for the day but for the morrow;

not merely for themselves but for mankind. A society so founded will, when nature favors, produce wealth and luxury for many. When those by-products come, they seem so good that they become promoted to be the all-sufficient end. Men are drawn away from long-range creative effort. They struggle to get and to hold material things.

When that happens in a national group that nation loses its soul. That is what has happened to us, and today we face the problem of how to regain that soul.

For guidance let us turn to Jesus Christ, who revealed to men not only the way of spiritual salvation but how to create a fellowship on earth. For that he sought for men four simple and very practical qualities: to see, to understand, to reason, and then to act.

Christ wanted men to see, to see far and to see truly. To get that kind of vision, he pointed out, requires avoidance of hypocrisies and group prejudices, which distort the vision and make men imagine they see what is not really there.

Christ wanted men to have hearts that comprehend the human significance of what is seen. That kind of heart requires, he pointed out, avoidance of material self-seeking which makes men hard and indifferent to all that cannot serve their selfish ends.

Christ wanted men to reason clearly and serenely. That requires, he pointed out, avoidance of evil emotions such as hatred and vengefulness, which enflame men's minds and distract them from the real problems that confront them.

Christ wanted men to act. He did not teach a purely contemplative religion. "Go" and "do" were his constant injunctions. "Let your light so shine before men, that they may see your good works."

If individuals today will follow these four simple precepts, then they will have found a way to lift themselves out of the state to which they have fallen. He who sees clearly, in whatever be his environment, who comprehends the human significance of what he sees, who thinks serenely what to do about it, and then does it, will find his action fruitful, probably far beyond his expectation. He will sense the power of creation and a satisfaction which far surpasses that of possession. He will become a person of righteous and creative faith.

If that happens, in sufficient numbers, then and only then can we as a nation resume a creative role in world affairs. Without that we are doomed. For the harmonious association of men is not achieved by treaties, or councils, or armies. These things may help. But the essential is that people find the way to do together works of creation. That way can never be found and followed by a nation unless it has first become the way of the individuals who make that nation's policy. There is no national being apart from you and me who can dream and hope and aspire. That is for men and women and children possessed of qualities unique to those whom God created to be but little lower than the angels. So if we would be a nation of creative faith, we must be individuals of creative faith.

Thus there devolves on every citizen a personal responsibility to develop in himself the qualities which we want to be characteristic of our nation.

When that has happened, our nation will again be a nation of vision. With that vision, we shall see a world in which most of humanity has been torn away from all established institutions. Almost everywhere a new society must be built. This is not only a calamity, it is an opportunity, the like of which men never saw before. So, if we see, we shall see the greatest challenge of all time.

We shall, as a nation, be comprehending. We shall hear the cry of multitudes that a way be found to save them and their children from the death, the misery, the starvation of body and soul which recurrent war and economic disorder now wreak upon man. We shall be so moved by that cry that we shall resolutely dedicate ourselves to find that way.

We shall, as a nation, think out the way to advance our purpose. The broad principles which need to be incorporated into the new world are not obscure. They involve practices which are widely followed as between men who live in personal contact with each other. Such practices now need world-wide application, because the world has grown so small. . . . To devise political machinery to implement these principles presents no insoluble problem. It needs only that we give our best thinking to that instead of to making some passing gain or satisfying some hate or prejudice.

Finally, we will act. We will not merely see the challenge, feel the sympathy, think out the way. We will act. We will embark, in company with others, on the next great adventure, that of building a fellowship that is world-wide in scope. Out of the perils, the difficulties, the accomplishments of that task, will come again the joy that is reserved to those who seek here to create in God's image.

8

Our Spiritual Heritage

THE PEOPLE of the United States have a great heritage. We are vaguely aware of it, but we are confused about its nature. To some it seems a material heritage. To others it seems a political heritage. It is, in its essentials, a religious heritage.

The founders of this nation were consciously launching a great experiment. It became widely known as an experiment in human freedom. So it was. But the experiment took that form because those who sponsored it were, for the most part, persons of deep religious faith. They were seeking to translate, into living reality, their spiritual convictions.

One of those convictions was that human beings are the children of God and as such endowed by him with certain inalienable rights. Since those rights are given by God, no men, however powerful or however numerous, can rightfully take them away from other men, even though those others be only weak or few.

Another of their basic convictions was that there are eternal principles of truth and righteousness which are reflected in a moral law. That law is one which all men can apprehend

---

Address at *New York Herald Tribune* Forum, October 21, 1947.

through their consciences, and it is a law which most men freely recognize as an obligation. It establishes a duty and a code of conduct so that the freedoms to which men are entitled will not be abused as license but will be used with respect for the general welfare.

A third basic conviction was that those who found a good way of life had a duty to help others to find the same way. The American experiment was never a purely selfish effort to get something exclusive for the American people. Our founders were imbued with a deep sense of mission. Their Declaration of Independence, as President Lincoln pointed out, was not a mere matter of the separation of the colonies from the motherland, but something "giving liberty, not alone to the people of this country, but hope for the world for all future time — it was that which gave promise that in due time the weights should be lifted from the shoulders of all men and that all should have an equal chance."

So it is that when today we ask ourselves what religion can contribute to man, we find some of the answers plainly written in our historical experience. As spiritual convictions have found vital expression, our nation has shown true greatness. As spiritual convictions have been feeble, we have lost in internal health and unity and our external prestige has declined. It is sure that if ever the unhappy day came when spiritual convictions were generally abandoned, then our great experiment in human freedom would ingloriously collapse.

The sovereignty of man rests upon a religious estimate of his nature. Without that estimate he tends to slavery.

A society of freedom cannot exist for long except on a foundation of belief that man is a child of God. If every human being does not contain within himself a spark of the Divine and a right to self-development in accordance with the dictates of his own conscience and of his own mind, then a society which dignifies the individual is purely a matter of expediency. It may be argued that a free society is the most expedient society because it is the most productive society. Certainly societies of freedom have, through their inventiveness, resourcefulness, and industriousness, developed a productivity never equaled by any society of dictatorship or despotism. But it is not possible to prove, merely on the basis of expediency, that a free society will for all time be the most productive society. Marxists concede the immense and superior productivity which the American system has achieved. But they contend that is merely a phase of history. They say that different forms of society are adapted to different times; that there was a time when slavery was the preferred form of society; then came serfdom; then came capitalism; now comes dictatorship of the proletariat as the next phase in a great historical progression.

There is no factual way to prove or disprove estimates of the future. But the Marxist thesis must be totally rejected if one accepts the religious view of the nature of man. Under that view, slavery, however expedient, was never right. Under that view, the despotism of a police state can never be right. It might be that a time would come when men would be more productive and more secure if they were treated as domesticated animals and driven to pasture and back to shelter under the direction of some superior human will. It is unnecessary to argue that point if one accepts, as did our forebears, the Christian view that man is destined to be more than a material producer and that his chief end is something more than physical security. The religious conception of the nature of man is the premise and the only premise from which political freedom surely follows.

But, also, freedom is indefensible if it stands alone. Freedom must be coupled with recognition of the moral law and of the fact that men's rights carry with them duties to fellow men. This nation was launched with emphasis upon individualism because the original environment was one which called for personal resourcefulness and pioneering. The satisfaction which comes from a sense of being creative then depended more on individual than on collective effort. But extreme individualism is no integral part of our religious heritage. The Jewish and Christian faiths have at all times emphasized the duty of man to his fellows, and that duty is a fundamental of our Christian faith. The moral law is sublimely reflected by the Ten Commandments and by the injunctions: "Thou shalt love the Lord thy God with all thy heart, and with all thy soul, and with all thy mind" and "Thou shalt love thy neighbor as thyself." Christ particularly emphasized these two commandments. Upon them, he said, "hang all the law and the prophets."

As any society matures and as its population becomes more dense and its economy more complex, love of neighbor is of increasing social significance. Then individual acts sharply affect others, and it is essential that, with respect to those acts, there should be a large measure of self-control and self-discipline and a sense of being a part of a combined effort to meet a common need. The joy of creation has to be derived more from joint efforts than from efforts which are isolated. Freedom becomes increasingly an opportunity for fellowship rather than an opportunity for private indulgence. If personal freedom is exercised without regard to the fate of others, then it becomes socially intolerable and, in fact, it will disappear. Broadly speaking, it can be said that unless a society is religious, it cannot be free. Without the disciplines of the moral law, freedom becomes chaotic and men accept the order of slavery.

A sense of mission is also needed if a society is to become and remain free. A people without a dynamic faith are constantly on the defensive, and that is a losing posture. But it is not enough to have a faith that is dynamic; that faith must be a righteous faith. Otherwise, it will break itself against the moral law. That law is no less a reality than is physical law, and its operation, though not always immediate, is inexorable.

Today some are frightened at the prospect of a world of strongly conflicting faiths. They fear that the consequence will be world turmoil, if not world war. Strident voices say that, for us, supineness is the recipe for peace.

There is indeed danger when men seek to make their faith prevail by methods of violence, coercion, and deceit. But these are not the methods of the Christian faith. Christ said: "Go ye into all the world, and preach the gospel to every creature" and "Let your light so shine before men, that they see your good works." A righteous faith prevails by appeal to the conscience and reason of men and by showing good fruits. Christians have learned, sometimes by their own bitter experience, that however good a faith may be, its proponents produce only ugly and evil things if they seek to promote their faith by methods of intolerance. That truth is a precious part of our spiritual and political heritage.

The American people must be resolved, and I am confident that they are resolved, to maintain that heritage. It makes senseless the fear, being recklessly spread, that for us to be strong in faith and works is to endanger the peace.

Freedom cannot be bought and peace cannot be had at the price of abandoning all faith that is dynamic. Those who preach that are either knaves or fools. What is essential is that men's faith should be a righteous faith, both in its substance and also in its means. Our society of freedom would quickly succumb to the overlordship of others if we renounced a sense of mission in the world. We would encounter unconquerable opposition if we sought to make our way prevail by might and not by merit. The need is for purposeful action inspired, in every aspect, by the ideals of the moral law.

Two thousand years ago Christ said: "The truth shall make you free" and "I am the way, the truth, and the life." Every one of those two thousand years sustains that utterance. The church spires which silhouette the skyline of America symbolize acceptance of his way. They point to a power above us from which derives our freedom.

9

Our Spiritual Need

SOMETHING has gone wrong with our nation, or we should not be in our present plight and mood. It is not like us to be on the defensive and to be fearful. That is new in our history.

The trouble is not material. We are establishing an all-time world record in the production of material things. What we lack is a righteous and dynamic faith. Without it, all else avails us little. The lack cannot be compensated for by politicians, however able; or by diplomats, however astute; or by scientists, however inventive; or by bombs, however powerful.

Once a people comes to feel dependent on material things, unfortunate consequences are inevitable.

At home, our institutions do not attract the spiritual loyalties needed for their defense. There is confusion in men's minds and corrosion of their souls. That makes our nation vulnerable to such hostile penetration as is illustrated by the spy activities so far revealed. No FBI, however efficient, can protect us under those circumstances.

Abroad, our foreign policies can be implemented only by

Chapter Twenty-one in John Foster Dulles, *War or Peace*. The Macmillan Company, 1950. Copyright, 1950, by John Foster Dulles.

money and goods. These are limited; and because they are limited, our policies are limited. Limited policies inevitably are defensive policies, and defensive policies inevitably are losing policies.

Today our military leaders define what they conceive to be strategic areas for military defense — perhaps the "North Atlantic area" as set forth in the North Atlantic Treaty. We draw a line which, like the Maginot Line, we then fortify as our defense.

Economists and budgetary experts, department heads and the Congress, calculate how much we can afford to give away in economic subsidies. The result may be, for example, $5,000,-000,000. Then we study to see where it can be spent to the best advantage, and, generally speaking, we spend it within the strategic area which the military have defined.

The result of this planning in military and economic terms is the staking out of a citadel, which we try to fortify and to provision. We have no affirmative policies beyond, for we cannot go farther with material things. Already we are straining our material resources to the limit, and we cannot greatly expand the scope of our policies if that means expanding our material expenditures. Regional policies, as expressed in the Rio Pact, the North Atlantic Pact, and the Truman Doctrine for Greece and Turkey, suggest that the Americas, Western Europe, and the Mediterranean mark the limits of our concern because they mark the limits of our immediate military and economic interests. We seem to have lost the spirit which animated Lincoln when he said of our Declaration of Independence that it gave "liberty, not alone to the people of this country, but hope for the world for all future time. It was that which gave promise that in due time the weights should be lifted from the shoulders of all men."

Up to the present, the American people have always had those qualities of the spirit that can be projected far beyond the limited reach of our material grasp. Those are the qualities that have made us great.

Our nation was founded as an experiment in human liberty. Its institutions reflected the belief of our founders that men had their origin and destiny in God; that they were endowed by him with inalienable rights and had duties prescribed by moral law, and that human institutions ought primarily to help men develop their God-given possibilities. We believed that if we built on that spiritual foundation, we should be showing men everywhere the way to a better and more abundant life.

We realized that vision. There developed here an area of spiritual, intellectual, and economic vigor the like of which the world had never seen. It was no exclusive preserve; indeed, world mission was a central theme. Millions were welcomed from other lands, to share equally the opportunities of the founders and their heirs. We put our experiment on public exhibition so that all might see and follow if they would. Through missionary activities and the establishment of schools and colleges, American ideals were carried throughout the world. We gave aid and comfort to those elsewhere who sought to follow in our way and to develop societies of greater human freedom.

That made it easy to conduct the foreign policy of the United States. In those days influence and opportunity abroad and security at home came naturally as by-products of what our people stood for in the world. Americans were welcomed everywhere because, it was judged, they were working in a common human cause. Our economic opportunities were not circumscribed by fears and jealousies such as penned in many others. We were the least militarized of any Western nation, yet, for a century, we were not endangered. No foreign ruler could have brought his people to try to destroy the "great American experiment" which they admired and the spiritual fruits of which they shared.

These conditions prevailed for one hundred years and more. Then, as our material power waxed, our spiritual power seemed to wane. We appeared to be less concerned with conducting a great experiment for the benefit of mankind and to be more concerned with piling up for ourselves material advantages. Our vision seemed to contract, and our sense of mission to lessen. Others began to think of us more as a possible source of money and material things and less as a source of inspiration and of guidance.

We have had to meet the severest test that can come to a people, the test of prosperity.

It was said by Jesus that material things will be added unto those who seek first the Kingdom of God and his righteousness. But when that happens, then comes the great trial. For, as Jesus warned, those material things can readily become the rust that corrodes men's souls.

Thus there is a familiar pattern. Men who feel a sense of duty to some higher Being strive here to do his will. Because of their faith, they have power and virtue and simple wisdom. They build not only for the day, but for the morrow; not merely for themselves, but for mankind. A society so founded will, when nature favors, produce wealth and luxury for many. When those by-products come, they seem so good that they become promoted to be the all-sufficient end. Men are drawn away from long-range creative effort. They struggle to get and to hold material things.

With that change comes ever growing danger. Americans

had security in the only way in which security can be assured, namely, as a by-product of great endeavor. When our endeavor lagged and we began to seek security as an end in itself, it more and more eluded us. It will always be that way. However rich we are, security cannot be bought at any money price. Five billions, or fifty billions, is not enough. Security and peace are not purchasable commodities. The Roman emperors in their declining days tried to buy peace, and the effort only whetted the appetites of those who sought to destroy them.

While our influence and security have been declining, those of Soviet Communism have been rising. That is not primarily due to the fact that Russia as a nation has great power, although the Red Army is a background threat. It is rather due to the fact that Soviet Communism has a creed, a creed of world-wide import. It is a creed in which the hard core of Party members believe fanatically, and which they are spreading with missionary zeal throughout the world.

There is no nook or cranny in all the world into which Communist influence does not penetrate. When the Politburo is making policies it does not say that there is no use having a policy for Guatemala or the Union of South Africa or the United States of Indonesia because they are too far away and cannot be reached either by the Red Army or by economic subsidy. Neither of these devices is the primary reliance of Soviet Communists in policy-making. They can and do implement policies with the portrayal of a "great Soviet Communist experiment" with which, during this century, they are catching the imagination of the people of the world, just as we did in the nineteenth century with our "great American experiment."

We know that that Communistic portrayal is a fraud and

a delusion. We know that Soviet Communists will not open their experiment at home to the test of free and impartial inspection. We know that those who are finally caught by the false lure of that portrayal quickly learn how different is the reality. The spider spins a beautiful web which shimmers in the sunlight, and he invites the fly into his parlor. Communist propaganda, like the spider's web, does attract. Once it has caught the people, despotism sucks them spiritually dry. But, as a prospect, Communism does have an appeal to the masses everywhere in Asia, in the islands of the Pacific, in South America, in Africa, and even in Western Europe.

The prestige of Soviet Communism in the world has been greatly increased by the fact that even in the West the Governments have adopted what, at first glance, seem to be basic parts of Soviet Communist doctrine.

Stalin said, "The strength and vitality of Marxism-Leninism lies in the fact that it does base its practical activity on the needs of the development of the material life of society."

Many non-Communist countries of the world, including indeed many "Christian" nations of the West, now seem to put primary emphasis upon developing "the material life of society" and to subordinate the spiritual development of the individual. The Communists cite that to prove that even the Western societies have had to adopt the materialistic thesis of Communism. The leaders in the West do not make any convincing denials, and the prestige of Soviet Communism in the world is greatly increased.

The difficulty is that we, ourselves, are unclear as to our faith and the relationship of that faith to our practices.

We can talk eloquently about liberty and freedom, and about human rights and fundamental freedoms, and about the dignity and worth of the human personality; but most of our vocabulary derives from a period when our own society was individualistic. Consequently, it has little meaning to those who live under conditions where individualism means premature death.

Also, we can talk eloquently about the material successes we have achieved, about the marvels of mass production, and about the number of automobiles, radios, and telephones owned by our people. That materialistic emphasis makes some feel that we are spiritually bankrupt. It makes others envious and more disposed to accept Communist glorification of "mass" effort to "develop the material life of society."

We are in a dilemma, and it is a grave dilemma. Because we have not resolved it, our spiritual influence in the world has waned, and we are tied down to the area that we can reach and influence by material things — guns and goods. That is why it is possible for our encirclement to proceed apace.

We cannot successfully combat Soviet Communism in the world and frustrate its methods of fraud, terrorism, and violence unless we have a faith with spiritual appeal that translates itself into practices which, in our modern, complex society, get rid of the sordid, degrading conditions of life in which the spirit cannot grow.

We are still unsure in our own minds where to look for solid ground between individualism and materialism. Our faith lacks the power and clear definition that would make it contagious in the world.

The religious faith of our founders emphasized individualism because the original environment called for personal resourcefulness and pioneering. Individual effort was the best way to get the satisfaction which comes from a sense of being creative. Also, individual creativeness was usually the means whereby society as a whole was most enriched.

But extreme individualism is no integral part of our religious heritage. The Jewish and Christian faiths have at all times emphasized the duty of man to his fellows; and that duty is fundamental in our religious faith. The moral law, the law of the prophets, is sublimely compressed into the two injunctions "Thou shalt love the Lord thy God" and "Thou shalt love thy neighbor as thyself."

There is an essential difference between a spiritual society and a materialistic society. The difference is not that the spiritual society is purely individualistic while the materialistic society is purely collectivist. It is not that the free society ignores material welfare while the materialistic society makes material welfare primary. The difference is that the spiritual society seeks material welfare by relying on and developing the individual's sense of duty to his fellow man and his willingness to exercise self-control and self-restraint in the discharge of that duty. The materialistic, irreligious society, which denies the existence of God or of a moral law, cannot depend upon love of God and love of neighbor. It must depend on governmental compulsion rather than on voluntary controls.

We have failed lamentably to see that we can get social justice without practicing atheism and materialism. It depends upon the willingness of the individual voluntarily to accept and discharge social obligations to his fellow man.

Because we have not seen that, many of our people have lost faith in a society of freedom. As a nation, although still religious, we have lost the connection between our religious faith and our practices. We keep religion and practices in separate compartments. We no longer see that our faith is relevant to modern conditions.

Once the connection between faith and works is broken, we can no longer generate a spiritual power that will flow throughout the world. The "conduct and example" of which our founders wrote are no longer a beacon light to those who live in the deep shadows cast by a mighty despotism. We have no message to send to the captive peoples to keep their hope and faith alive.

We must change all that. We can, and must, reject totally the Marxian thesis that material things are primary and spiritual things only secondary. Slavery and despotism, even if they seem expedient, can never be right. We must not be afraid to recapture faith in the primacy of human liberty and freedom, and to hold to the religious view that man is destined by God to be more than a material producer, and that his chief end is something more than physical security. We must believe that men everywhere ought to be released from the spiritual, intellectual, economic, and political strait jackets into which they are increasingly being put on the theory that this will improve the material welfare of the social group to which they belong.

Equally, we must clearly see that a society of freedom is not a society of un-co-ordinated self-seeking individuals. It is a society that is co-ordinated. But the bonds are primarily the bonds of fellowship which derive from belief that men are destined to be brothers through the Fatherhood of God, that each man is his brother's keeper, and that we should love our neighbors as ourselves.

That belief translates itself into a society of individuals who love God and their fellow man, and who fear only God and not any man; who work hard as a matter of duty and self-satisfaction, not compulsion; who gain personal and family security primarily through ability and willingness voluntarily to earn and save; who are self-reliant, resourceful, and adaptable to changing conditions, and for whom life is not merely physical growth and enjoyment, but intellectual and spiritual development. It also translates itself into public organizations, through which men willingly co-operate, at national and local levels, to do what they cannot well do otherwise.

But governmental authority at all times and places is limited by the principle that governmental action expresses, but does not replace, voluntary acceptance of social responsibility. Government action must stop short of seeming to shift social responsibility from the individual to the government.

That limitation on governmental power makes some imperfections inevitable. The existence of imperfections does not prove that the system is wrong, and it need not make us feel ashamed or defeated. In a sense, the existence of flaws proves that the system is right. Human nature at best is imperfect, and any system which is based on human nature is bound to have defects. The only system that is theoretically flawless is one of absolute despotism, "unlimited power, based on force and not on law" (Stalin). Then, in theory, all disharmonies, all imperfections can be removed, all grit can quickly be cleaned out, and perfect mechanical harmony can result. However, the attempt to do that creates moral enormities. That is always the case when men indulge in the conceit that they can do better than God.

Our greatest need is to regain confidence in our spiritual heritage. Religious belief in the moral nature and possibilities of man is, and must be, relevant to every kind of society, throughout the ages past and those to come. It is relevant to the complex conditions of modern society. We need to see that, if we are to combat successfully the methods and practices of a materialistic belief.

There is no use having more and louder Voices of America unless we have something to say that is more persuasive than anything that has yet been said.

To find that message is, above all, a task for the spiritual leaders of our nation. In finding it they can contribute, and contribute decisively, to the peaceful frustration of the evil methods and designs of Soviet Communism.

Many preachers and educators bemoan the fact that scientific knowledge has greatly advanced man's capacity to do harm. We must not believe that new knowledge is, of itself, something to be shunned. Great material power is dangerous in an age of materialism. It is not dangerous in an age of spiritualism. New scientific knowledge is dangerous today because it comes at a time when spiritual leadership has failed to make clear the connection between belief and practice. It is more important to advance the spiritual clock than to try to stop or set back the scientific clock.

President Wilson, in an article written a few weeks before he died, reviewed the threat of the revolutionary doctrines and practices of Communism. He concluded: "The sum of the whole matter is this, that our civilization cannot survive materially unless it be redeemed spiritually. . . . Here is the final challenge to our churches, to our political organizations, and to our capitalists — to everyone who fears God or loves his country."

10

Morals and Power

S INCE I have been Secretary of State, I have been to Europe, the Near East, and South Asia. Before that, in connection with negotiating the Japanese peace treaty, I had an excellent chance to get a firsthand look at our foreign representatives in Japan, Korea, and other parts of the Far East.

One of the things that most impressed me in these areas was the down-to-earth co-operation which existed between our civilian and military officials. . . .

◇◇◇◇

It is teamwork between the military and civilian which has given us the necessary strength whenever and wherever we have needed it.

I should like to talk for a few minutes about power in a material sense, such as is represented by our splendid military establishment. What is the purpose of this power? Admiral Mahan is credited with one of the best answers to this question. It is that the role of power is to give moral ideas the time to take root. Where moral ideas already are well rooted, there is little occasion for much military or police force. We see that

Address at the graduation exercises of the National War College, June 16, 1953.

illustrated in our own communities. Where the people accept the moral law and its great commandments, where they exercise self-control and self-discipline, then there is very little need for police power. Under these circumstances, it is sufficient to have a very modest force to take care of the small minority, always found in every community, which disregards the precepts of the moral law.

Where, however, there are many who do not accept moral principles, then that creates the need of force to protect those who do. That, unfortunately, is the case in the world community of today.

At the present time, there is no moral code which has worldwide acceptance. The principles upon which our society is based — the principles which we believe to be both humanitarian and just — are not accepted by governments which dominate more than one third of mankind.

The result is that we have a world which is, for the most part, split between two huge combinations. On the one hand, there is the United States and its free-world associates. This is a voluntary alliance of free peoples working together in the recognition that without unity there could be catastrophe.

On the other hand, there is the totalitarian bloc led by the Soviet Union — an artificial, imposed unity which cannot be called an alliance in the sense that we use the word.

These huge concentrations are in conflict because each reflects differing aims, aspirations, and social, political, and economic philosophies. We must assume that they will continue to remain in basic conflict, in one way or another, until such time as the Communists so change their nature as to admit that those who wish to live by the moral law are free to do so without coercion by those who believe in enforced conformity to a materialistic standard.

This is one of the hard facts of international existence which we must accept. We cannot close our eyes to it. It will not go away simply because we hope that it will do so.

We must plan accordingly. . . .

◇◇◇◇

What makes the Soviet Union — the fountain-head of world communism — act as it does? Why do the Soviets seek power and more power?

These complex questions are not simply answered. There are many forces which motivate the Soviet drive for power. Among those forces are these which I should like to mention: ideology, the historic imperialistic urge, and the chronic insecurity complex which besets those who rule by force.

◇◇◇◇

This picture which I have given of the international situation is not a pleasing one. It does not hold out the prospect of any quick change for the better or any early elimination of our need for power in order to permit moral principles to take root rather than be uprooted.

However, if we do maintain power, and if we do subject it to moral law and use it truly to enable moral principles to survive, and thrive, and spread in the world, we can have hope in the future. For we know that in the long run the fruits of a spiritual faith prevail over the fruits of materialism.

The great weakness of Soviet Communist doctrine is that it denies morality. That is its Achilles heel, of which we must take advantage. We can take advantage of it if — but only if — we ourselves accept the supremacy of moral law.

Our nation was founded by men who believed that there was a divine Creator who endowed men with inalienable rights. They believed, as George Washington put it in his Farewell Address, that religion and morality are the great pillars of human happiness and that morality cannot prevail in exclusion of religious principles.

Our Federal and State Constitutions, our laws and practices, reflect the belief that there is a Being superior to ourselves who has established his own laws which can be comprehended by all human beings and that human practices should seek conformity with those laws.

Seeking first the Kingdom of God and his righteousness, many material things were added to us. We developed here an area of spiritual, intellectual, and material richness, the like of which the world has never seen. What we did caught the imagination of men everywhere and became known everywhere as the "great American experiment." Our free society became a menace to every despot because we showed how to meet the hunger of the people for greater opportunity and for greater dignity. The tide of despotism, which at that time ran high, was rolled back and we ourselves enjoyed security.

We need to recapture that mood.

Today some seem to feel that Americanism means being tough and "hard-boiled," doing nothing unless we are quite sure that it is to our immediate short-term advantage, boasting of our own merit and seeing in others only demerit.

That is a caricature of America. Our people have always been generous to help, out of their abundance, those who are the victims of misfortune. Our forebears have traditionally had what the Declaration of Independence refers to as a decent respect for the opinion of mankind. They sought to practice the golden rule by doing to others as they would have others do unto them. Their conduct and example made our nation one that was respected and admired throughout the world.

So, in conclusion, I say to you who graduate from the National War College: Be proud of your association with U.S.

power, which is indispensable in the world today; but remember that that power is worthy only as it is the shield behind which moral values are invigorated and spread their influence; and accept, as citizens, the obligation to preserve and enhance those moral values. They are the rich heritage that has been bequeathed us. It must be our ambition that future generations shall look back upon us, as we look back upon those who preceded us, with gratitude for the gift to our republic of the qualities that make it noble, so that men call it blessed.

III

*The Spiritual Foundations
of World Order*

As we have noted, at the Oxford Conference on "Church, Community, and State" in July, 1937, Mr. Dulles' estimate of the influence that the churches might exert in the furtherance of peace and world order underwent a radical reversal. His previous attitude of skepticism and aloofness gave way to admiration and hopefulness. From then on, he joined actively in Christian concern with international issues.

He participated in an International Conference of Lay Experts and Ecumenical Leaders convened by the Provisional Committee of the World Council of Churches in Geneva in August, 1939, on the very eve of World War II. His mind and pen are evident in its notable Memorandum, which sought less to forestall a conflict that, by then, was clearly inescapable than to define the relations that should be maintained between Christians in nations at war and to outline some of the principles that should determine the eventual peace.

When war finally broke, he gave prodigally of time and energy to attempt to stir and inform the consciences of churchmen and, through them, of the American people on the character of the peace that should follow. In 1940, a Commission to Study the Bases of a Just and Durable Peace was formed under Mr. Dulles' chairmanship. Its purposes were set forth in his Foreword to one of its earliest publications:

"The American people face grave alternatives. Shall we continue to be a people without a faith, contenting ourselves with ceaseless and exhausting combat against alien faiths? Or will we develop a faith of our own? If so, will that faith be a righteous faith or an evil faith?

"Upon the answers to these questions will depend the kind of world in which we and our children will live.

"This book has been written as part of the effort of our Commission to assure a faith that will be righteous and that, because it is righteous, can be shared by other peoples and lead to just and durable peace.

"We realize that to achieve a righteous faith calls for spiritual leadership of increased intensity. It is our hope that some of the thoughts here expressed will produce that leadership. None are too humble to achieve it. That is one of our objectives. Our other purpose is to assure a general level of thinking that will make easier the task of Christian leadership and which will make it impossible for evil faiths to take root among us. That calls for education. All who take part in it will help to shape our destiny."

From that time until he was called to Washington as adviser to President Roosevelt's Administration in 1945, a very considerable proportion of Mr. Dulles' effort was channeled through this Commission. Under his guidance, it issued a series of documents and proposals that received wide attention and exerted marked influence. It sponsored and organized consultations and conferences, in which he was often a leader. Although its statements seldom bore his name, his was always the major hand in their authorship, and, since they were commended by him as Chairman, they may be recognized as expressing his views. One is included in this collection of his writings. His own extensive speaking, whether before church or secular gatherings, reiterated his convictions on the moral and spiritual prerequisites for world order.

After 1945 he was able to give less constant attention to the Commission's work, but he continued to maintain close contact. In the summer of 1947 he went to Cambridge, England, to preside over the international meeting that created the Commission of the Churches on International Affairs, of which he was Vice-Chairman. In the postwar period, he continued to set forth substantially the same principles essential to a "just and durable peace."

11

The Need for a Righteous Faith

THIS paper forms part of an effort by the churches to assure peace which will be just and durable. Many question the timing of our effort. They urge that our thoughts should be of nothing beyond military victory and our emotions only those hot ones which, they conceive, best feed the flames of war.

The challenge is one that must be met. I do not doubt that it can be met, for what we seek for the American people is nothing that will prove a weakness. Rather, we seek that strength which is to be found only in the propulsion of a deep faith and sense of high mission in the world. I assert that:

1. It is our lack of impelling faith that has weakened us and encouraged the development elsewhere of the evils which now imperil us;

2. The primitive emotions, such as anger, hatred, and vengefulness, are no substitutes for the faith that makes men strong. Such emotions are false stimulants which weaken men by burning out their moral fiber;

3. The goals which can inspire us to great endeavor are to

Opening chapter in the pamphlet *A Righteous Faith for a Just and Durable Peace,* published by the Commission of the Churches on a Just and Durable Peace, October, 1942.

be found by having and using the qualities which Christ taught. We need visions that see clear, minds that think straight, and hearts that are comprehending. If, then, we act under such directives, there will be rekindled in us a sense of creative purpose that will make us strong.

During the period of one hundred and twenty-five years which preceded the First World War, the French, the British, and the American nations were imbued with and radiated great faiths. These were partly good and partly bad, but at least they served to make these nations the three great powers of the world. The spirit of the French Revolution, with its slogan of "Liberty, Equality, and Fraternity," changed the face of the Western world. It inspired the birth of democratic processes and it created widespread admiration and sympathy for France. In England, the Industrial Revolution opened up a new economic era. Its consequences were carried into the uttermost parts of the earth through an imperial policy sought to be given moral sanction as a carrying of the "white man's burden." Hundreds of millions of people became politically and economically related to Britain, and, by and large, their material and social status was thereby greatly improved. We, in the United States, became conscious of a "manifest destiny" under the impulse of which we opened up a vast continent. We, too, sometimes used reprehensible methods, but we fashioned here a new freedom for millions of repressed persons from other lands. Another faith which burned bright in Britain and the United States was a religious faith. It found expression in missionary efforts which profoundly influenced the moral fabric of much of the world. Wherever trading posts sprang up, there, too, was a mission post. Thus we balanced the materialistic motives which dominated much of economic penetration.

The close of the First World War seems to have marked an exhaustion of our spiritual springs. The French, the British, and ourselves emerged as burnt-out peoples. In the United States, there was a quick descent from the lofty motives that had made so notable a contribution to victory. In all three countries postwar efforts were concentrated upon searching for "security." We had nothing to give. We had no fire to impart. Those few in Germany and Japan who sought after the war to carry there the torch of democracy received no help from us. We wanted merely to be left alone, and in our isolated and, as we thought, "matured" economies, we found little to do except to squabble over the partition of the material wealth we had theretofore created. Upon the world there descended a spirit of disillusionment and discouragement. The youth were without opportunity or hope, the workers were without employment, and the aged were without security. All were without faith.

It is, of course, impossible to perpetuate a spiritual vacuum. So it inevitably came about that here and there, throughout the world, new faiths were born. . . . These faiths were largely repugnant to us. . . . But, good or bad, they were faiths for which men were eager to sacrifice and, if need be, die. We have been startled by what those nations have performed.

From all this I deduce that we, too, need a faith, a faith that will make us strong, a faith so profound that we, too, will feel that we have a mission to spread it through the world. Today we have it not. The American people believe in nothing with conviction. We are cynical and disillusioned. Even our war effort we look upon primarily as one of resistance, not of accomplishment; and victory as being that which will assure our being left alone.

Such a spiritual state is conducive neither to a military victory nor, when victory is won, to subsequent peace. For again new faiths will arise to attack us, and in the long run we will succumb. The impact of the dynamic upon the static — while it may be resisted in detail — will ultimately destroy that which it attacks. The First World War, this World War, and the next world war will go down in history as a series of rearguard actions by disillusioned peoples who, equipped only with the material products of past greatness, sought valiantly but vainly to resist the penetration of alien faiths.

At this critical period in our national life we are told that we should not waste time in seeking to arouse in the American people a sense of great purpose in the world. It is best, they say, that we think only of military victory and that we seek to promote it by generating anger, hatred, vengefulness, and self-righteousness.

There are, of course, those who must concentrate upon the immediate prosecution of the war. That is peculiarly true of our combat and production task forces. But the vast remainder of us are, too, a task force, our task being to dedicate our nation to long-range purposes of human welfare. Thereby alone can we compensate the sacrifices that war will exact. Thereby alone can we give the youth who must die the sense of accomplishing more than the gallant performance of cold duty. Thereby alone can we assure that out of this war will be born an impetus that will carry through victory into an era of creative peace.

Christians, if they be true, must seek to discharge this task, whatever the world may say. For Christ's whole ministry taught the subordinate role of immediate material objectives. He sought to inculcate in men a spiritual power which would turn earthly events, whether labeled "victory" or "defeat," into an increased doing of God's will on earth.

I recall that Christ ministered at a time when international and social problems existed in aggravated form. The relations of the nations were determined by force, and much of the world lived under the heel of a military dictator. Slavery was a generally accepted institution. In the face of that situation Christ did not devote himself to achieving specific reforms. The reason surely was not indifference to the evils and human misery that surrounded him. Must it not have been that to have effected such reforms in the social structure of his time would have been of but passing value? He sought rather to show men how, throughout the ages, they might find the way to surmount evil, which could constantly be reappearing in ever-changing form. That way, he taught, was for men to act out of visions that would see clear, minds that would think straight, and hearts that would comprehend the essential unity and equal worthiness of all human beings. He inveighed against hatred and vengefulness, self-conceit and deification of one's particular nation, race, or class. He did so not only because such emotions are repugnant to God's will for man, but also because they always make men incompetent to deal with human problems. They create those blind masses and those blind leaders who, he pointed out, end up together in the pit.

Because many are afraid to trust Christ, I cite the example of temporal leaders acting in their political capacities.

Of what did the greatness of Lincoln consist? It was that he rejected hatred and vengefulness as the stimulant of war effort. He pleaded that there be malice toward none, and found in great moral and political truths the armor of righteousness. I cite, also, the contemporary example of Mr. Roosevelt and Mr. Churchill. When they met on the Atlantic they sought to use that dramatic occasion to advance to the utmost the cause to which their nations were committed. What was the way they elected? It was to compose and to proclaim the Atlantic Charter. Thereby they sought to achieve that moral leadership which they recognized as an essential ingredient of victory.

The Atlantic Charter was no hysterical call for victory as an end in itself. There is not in it a word which evokes hatred, vengefulness, and the deification of our own nations. It portrays, calmly, the better world we seek. And that world is one of greater opportunity for all men everywhere, victor and vanquished alike.

I cite, finally, the example of the Axis Powers. To the extent that they were propelled by a sense of constructive achievement, their peoples were unified and made strong. But because their faiths were shot through with evil, evil men readily came to leadership, and these have increasingly invoked hatred, vengefulness, cruelty, and lust. Thereby the moral strength of their peoples has deteriorated, resistance has constantly mounted, their victories have proved illusory, and ultimate failure is inevitable.

We can, therefore, be confident that in following Christ we are not jeopardizing the welfare of our nation. The stimulation that comes from hatred and vengefulness is like the stimulation produced by drugs and alcohol. There is created, to be sure, a sense of fervor. But that sense is false. Actually such emotions make neither for competence nor for sustained power. They confuse the thinking, blur the vision, and burn out the souls of those who rely upon them. They arouse, in others, a resistance which makes victory more difficult to achieve, and renders it illusory if, finally, it be achieved. Such emotions are no substitute, either in war or peace, for a sense of identification with some great creative purpose.

How are we to achieve a sense of mission and of great purpose? Our answer is: by action based upon seeing, understanding, and thinking. We urge that men clarify their vision so that they may see truly the world in which they live; that they purify their spirits so that they may be comprehending; that they free their minds of paralyzing emotions so that they may be competent. We then ask for action. Out of action directed by such qualities of vision, of soul, of mind, will be born the faith that will make us strong.

1. If we have vision, what is it we shall see? We shall, like Christ, see a multitude who hunger. That multitude is all about us — some near, some afar. They hunger not only for things material but for things spiritual. We would not be seeing truly if we saw only material wants. Such needs exist and they are great. But the greatest need is not for things. Men hunger for sympathy and fellowship and hope. They want education and the possibility of mental pursuits which will lift them out of their physical environment. They crave the vibrant thrill which comes from creative effort. They need a religious faith which will carry them through tribulations which no material wealth can prevent.

Christ saw and taught that material things served chiefly as vehicles for bringing into being those nonmaterial values that men need most. When he told the rich young man to give all to the poor, he saw, not so much the material advantage for the poor as the value of the spiritual outlook that would prompt such an act. By similar standards he appraised the widow's gift of her mites and Mary's sacrifice of her precious ointment.

So it is that as our eyes are opened we will see material

needs, but we will see them in subordinate relationship to spiritual needs.

2. If we have hearts that are comprehending, we shall, like Christ, be moved with compassion. We shall hear the cry of the masses that a way be found to save them and their children from the death, the misery, the starvation of body and soul which recurrent war and economic disorder now wreak upon man. We shall be so moved by that cry that we shall resolutely dedicate ourselves to the achievement of a better order. We shall find, in that dedication, something that will make our own lives worth living and our own nation worth preserving.

3. If we have minds that function, we shall find ways to advance our purpose and to assure that we, and others, may have life and have it more abundantly. The broad principles that should govern our international conduct are not obscure. They grow out of the practice by the nations of the simple things Christ taught. . . . Such principles mark the channels into which our minds must direct our international acts if they are to be productive of permanent good.

We have already, in politics, learned much of how to organize large units of society so that those within them will live at peace with each other. We have not thought out, however, how to carry such principles forward into the international field. We have already, in economics, learned how to create tools and harness natural forces, so that today the effort of a human being can be multiplied one hundredfold. There is no lack of the natural bounty with which God endowed the earth. There is no technical or material obstacle to achieving a constantly expanding measure of both production and consumption. We still have not learned, however, how to construct an economic machine which will not blight those spiritual values which man needs most.

To create political organs of international operation, to make economics our servant, not our master, calls for minds that function free of the paralyzing emotions that Christ condemned.

4. Finally, we must act. Christ did not teach a purely contemplative religion — "Let your light so shine before men, that they may see your good works." We must not feel impotent until there has been developed some great and all-inclusive pattern of a perfected world order. The essential is to develop in ourselves a sense of creative power and purpose. That can be achieved out of a series of acts which, of themselves, may be nonspectacular. If such acts are born out of clear vision, human comprehension, and intelligence, we will be surprised by the fruitful consequences of what we thus do. Inspired and propelled by those consequences, we will steadily move forward, enlarging the practical expression of our faith and developing for it a defined and expanding pattern. The Delaware Conference noted, as illustrating the type of international action which should even now be begun, certain proposals of our Government designed to effectuate the "good neighbor" policy and to work out the obligations of allied nations under "lend lease." Those pronouncements, if translated into reality, seemed to us to be national acts of enlightened self-interest of the kind that might start us in ways of creative purpose. Even in the midst of war there exist ample opportunities for action which will rekindle a sense of power to accomplish a great mission in the world. As our national faith thus grows and is made manifest by works, its influence will be contagious throughout the world. As the evil faiths that combat us collapse, leaving death and ruin as their fruit, the faith that makes us strong will encompass the earth. It will unite men, as

never before, in common and constructive purpose.

This war is often called a war of survival. We must make it more than that, for survival, of itself, is a barren thing. Let us conceive of this war as a war for opportunity, for the chance to become a positive force for human betterment. Only thus will we be infused with spiritual power that will make us strong, whether for victory or for peace. It is that strength — not a weakness — that we seek.

12

Moral and Spiritual Bases for a Just and Lasting Peace

As MEMBERS of the Christian church, we seek to view all problems of world order in the light of the truth concerning God, man, and God's purpose for the world made known in Jesus Christ. We believe that the eternal God revealed in Christ is the Ruler of men and of nations and that his purpose in history will be realized. For us he is the source of moral law and the power to make it effective.

From this faith Christians derive the ethical principles upon which world order must be based. These principles, however, seem to us to be among those which men of good will everywhere may be expected to recognize as part of the moral law. In this we rejoice. For peace will require the co-operation of men of all nations, races, and creeds. We have therefore first set out (Points 1 to 9) those guiding principles which, it seems to us, Christians and non-Christians alike can accept.

We believe that a special responsibility rests upon the people of the United States. We accordingly (Point 10) express our thoughts in that regard.

Above all, we are impressed by the supreme responsibility

Adopted by the Federal Council of the Churches of Christ in America, December, 1942.

which rests upon Christians. Moral law may point the way to peace, but Christ, we believe, showed that way with greatest clarity. We therefore, in conclusion (Points 11 and 12), address ourselves to Christians.

GUIDING PRINCIPLES

1

WE BELIEVE that moral law, no less than physical law, undergirds our world. There is a moral order which is fundamental and eternal, and which is relevant to the corporate life of men and the ordering of human society. If mankind is to escape chaos and recurrent war, social and political institutions must be brought into conformity with this moral order.

2

WE BELIEVE that the sickness and suffering which afflict our present society are proof of indifference to, as well as direct violation of, the moral law. All share in responsibility for the present evils. There is none who does not need forgiveness. A mood of genuine penitence is therefore demanded of us — individuals and nations alike.

3

WE BELIEVE that it is contrary to the moral order that nations in their dealings with one another should be motivated by a spirit of revenge and retaliation. Such attitudes will lead, as they always have led, to renewed conflict.

4

WE BELIEVE that the principle of co-operation and mutual concern, implicit in the moral order and essential to a just and durable peace, calls for a true community of nations. The interdependent life of nations must be ordered by agencies having the duty and the power to promote and

safeguard the general welfare of all peoples. Only thus
can wrongs be righted and justice and security be achieved.
A world of irresponsible, competing, and unrestrained national sovereignties, whether acting alone or in alliance or
in coalition, is a world of international anarchy. It must
make place for a higher and more inclusive authority.

5

WE BELIEVE that economic security is no less essential than
political security to a just and durable peace. Such security
nationally and internationally involves among other things
the use of material resources and the tools of production to
raise the general standard of living. Nations are not economically self-sufficient, and the natural wealth of the
world is not evenly distributed. Accordingly, the possession
of such natural resources should not be looked upon as an
opportunity to promote national advantage or to enhance
the prosperity of some at the expense of others. Rather,
such possession is a trust to be discharged in the general
interest. This calls for more than an offer to sell to all on
equal terms. Such an offer may be a futile gesture unless
those in need can, through the selling of their own goods
and services, acquire the means of buying. The solution
of this problem, doubtless involving some international organization, must be accepted as a responsibility by those
who possess natural resources needed by others.

6

WE BELIEVE that international machinery is required to facilitate the easing of such economic and political tensions
as are inevitably recurrent in a world which is living and
therefore changing. Any attempt to freeze an order of
society by inflexible treaty specifications is bound, in the
long run, to jeopardize the peace of mankind. Nor must

it be forgotten that refusal to assent to needed change may be as immoral as the attempt by violent means to force such change.

7

WE BELIEVE that that government which derives its just powers from the consent of the governed is the truest expression of the rights and dignity of man. This requires that we seek autonomy for all subject and colonial peoples. Until that shall be realized, the task of colonial government is no longer one of exclusive national concern. It must be recognized as a common responsibility of mankind, to be carried out in the interests of the colonial peoples by the most appropriate form of organization. This would, in many cases, make colonial government a task of international collaboration for the benefit of colonial peoples who would, themselves, have a voice in their government. As the agencies for the promotion of world-wide and economic security become effective, the moral, social and material welfare of colonial populations can be more fully realized.

8

WE BELIEVE that military establishments should be internationally controlled and be made subject to law under the community of nations. For one or more nations to be forcibly deprived of their arms while other nations retain the right of maintaining or expanding their military establishments can only produce an uneasy peace for a limited period. Any initial arrangement which falls short of this must therefore be looked upon as temporary and provisional.

9

WE BELIEVE that the right of all men to pursue work of their own choosing and to enjoy security from want and op-

pression is not limited by race, color, or creed. The rights
and liberties of racial and religious minorities in all lands
should be recognized and safeguarded. Freedom of religious worship, of speech and assembly, of the press, and
of scientific inquiry and teaching are fundamental to human development and in keeping with the moral order.

10

WE BELIEVE that, in bringing international relations into conformity with the moral law, a very heavy responsibility devolves upon the United States. For at least a generation
we have held preponderant economic power in the world,
and with it the capacity to influence decisively the shaping
of world events. It should be a matter of shame and hu-
miliation to us that actually the influences shaping the
world have largely been irresponsible forces. Our own positive influence has been impaired because of concentration
on self and on our short-range material gains. Many of the
major preconditions of a just and durable peace require
changes of national policy on the part of the United States.
Among such may be mentioned: equal access to natural
resources, economic collaboration, equitable treatment of
racial minorities, international control of tariffs, limitation
of armaments, participation in world government. We
must be ready to subordinate immediate and particular national interests to the welfare of all. If the future is to be
other than a repetition of the past, the United States must
accept the responsibility for constructive action commensurate with its power and opportunity.

11

WE BELIEVE that, as Christian citizens, we must seek to translate our beliefs into practical realities and to create a public
opinion which will insure that the United States shall

play its full and essential part in the creation of a moral way of international living. We must strive within the life of our own nation for change which will result in the more adequate application here of the principles above enumerated as the basis for a just and durable world order.

12

WE BELIEVE that a supreme responsibility rests with the church. The church, being a creation of God in Jesus Christ, is called to proclaim to all men everywhere the way of life. Moreover, the church, which is now in reality a world community, may be used of God to develop his spirit of righteousness and love in every race and nation and thus to make possible a just and durable peace. For this service Christians must now dedicate themselves, seeking forgiveness for their sins and the constant guidance and help of God, upheld by faith that the kingdoms of this world shall become the Kingdom of Christ and that he shall reign forever and ever.

STATEMENT OF POLITICAL PROPOSITIONS

INTRODUCTORY STATEMENT BY THE COMMISSION

It seems to have been reserved to the people of this country, by their conduct and example, to decide whether societies of men are really capable or not of establishing good government from reflection and choice, or whether they are forever destined to depend for their political constitutions on accident and force. The crisis at which we are arrived may be regarded as the era in which that decision is to be made, and a wrong election of the part we shall act may deserve to be considered as the general misfortune of mankind.
                              —THE FEDERALIST, 1787.

The American people again find themselves in an era of critical decision. It must now be determined, this time in world-wide terms, whether men are capable of establishing good government from reflection and choice, or whether they will continue to be buffeted about by force and by accident. Now, as before, it is reserved to the people of this country to play a decisive role. Now, more than ever, a wrong choice of the part we shall act will involve us in the general misfortune of mankind.

In anticipation of this critical period, the Federal Council of Churches, over two years ago, set up this Commission to Study the Bases of a Just and Durable Peace. We have diligently pursued that study. We have seen and said that the ills which afflict our society are fundamentally due to nonconformity with a moral order, the laws of which are as imperative

---

Issued by the Commission to Study the Bases of a Just and Durable Peace, March, 1943.

and as inexorable as are those that order our physical world. Indifference to and violation of these moral laws always bring such sickness and suffering as today afflict mankind. We have, in a Statement of Guiding Principles, set down certain principles of that moral order as being particularly relevant to our times and to our national responsibility and opportunity. That Statement has been officially endorsed by the Federal Council of Churches, and the widespread response which it has evoked from Christian people makes it clear that they predominantly hold the beliefs therein set forth.

Many now ask, What shall we do?

The first and paramount task of the Christian churches remains that of bringing more persons to subject their lives to the will of God as revealed in Jesus Christ. For us he is the source of the moral law of which we speak. He is the source of moral judgments on the issues of this war upon which the Federal Council of Churches has also spoken. Only if the Christian churches of this land build a spiritual foundation that is broad and deep, will this nation pursue righteous policies. Only if spiritual revelation strike from our eyes the scales of hatred, hypocrisy, intolerance, and greed, will we be competent to cope with the immensely difficult problems that confront us.

But there is a secondary task to which our Commission can now properly address itself. That is to point out that the Guiding Principles we have proclaimed compel certain broad political conclusions. We do that now because the course of events is such that a time for action is at hand.

Military peril has dramatized, for all to see, the need for international co-operation. But as military victory becomes more certain and draws more near, that need will be less obvious. As we come to grips with the appalling moral, social, and material aftermaths of Axis rule, transitory issues will arise to perplex and divide the United Nations. These may loom large and obscure the fundamentals and incline us to relapse into reliance only upon our own strength. Thus, if our nation does not make the right choice soon, it may never be made in our time.

We have, accordingly, now formulated and we present herewith a Statement of Political Propositions that flow from the moral principles we have heretofore enunciated.

We have stated our Propositions in simple and minimum terms. We recognize that as so stated there is much latitude as to their form and detailed content and as to the timing of their full realization. These matters are important, and their determination will involve much honest difference of opinion which, ultimately, must be reconciled. But the Propositions, as stated by us, serve to force the initial and vital decision on the direction in which this nation will move. They force that decision in relation to six major areas within which the factual interdependence of the world has become such as to require political mechanism for co-operative action. If the six Propositions we enunciate become an official program of this nation, we will be committed to move, by definite steps, to bring ourselves into an ordered relationship with others. Only if the nations join to do this, can we escape chaos and recurrent war. Only if the United States assumes a leadership, can it be done now. For we, more than any other nation, have the capacity to influence decisively the shaping of world events. . . .

◇◇◇◇

The many who believe the things we believe and who desire, as citizens, to do something about it, have here a field for action.

—JOHN FOSTER DULLES, Chairman

POLITICAL PROPOSITIONS

I

The peace must provide the political framework for a continuing collaboration of the United Nations and, in due course, of neutral and enemy nations.

II

The peace must make provision for bringing within the scope of international agreement those economic and financial acts of national governments which have widespread international repercussions.

III

The peace must make provision for an organization to adapt the treaty structure of the world to changing underlying conditions.

IV

The peace must proclaim the goal of autonomy for subject peoples, and it must establish international organization to assure and to supervise the realization of that end.

V

The peace must establish procedures for controlling military establishments everywhere.

VI

The peace must establish in principle, and seek to achieve in practice, the right of individuals everywhere to religious and intellectual liberty.

13

World Brotherhood Through the State

IT IS not easy these days to talk about the brotherhood of nations. It would have been easier a year or two ago. Then there was a brotherhood in arms. Now that brotherhood has given way to strain and tension.

War coalitions usually fall apart when they have destroyed the common peril. This time, however, what is happening is more than that. We seem to be witnessing a challenge to established civilization — the kind of thing which occurs only once in centuries.

In the tenth century after Christ the so-called Christian world was challenged by an alien faith. The tide of Islam flowed from Arabia and swept over much of Christendom. It was not primarily a military thrust. Rather, it was a social challenge. H. G. Wells said of it: "Islam prevailed because it was the best social and political order the times could offer. It prevailed because everywhere it found politically apathetic peoples and selfish and unsound governments, out of touch with any people at all. . . . It offered better terms than any other to the mass of mankind."

Address under the auspices of The Brotherhood of St. Andrew, Convention Hall, Philadelphia, Sunday, September 8, 1946.

Now another ten centuries have rolled by, and the accumulated civilization of those centuries is faced with another challenge. This time the challenger is Soviet Communism.

The faith and institutions of Soviet Communism differ vastly from those of the Western democracies. The official creed of the Party is an abstruse materialism. The form of government is dictatorship. The economic life is an extreme form of state socialism. The official methods are ruthless and intolerant. The spirit is revolutionary. The scope of its effort is universal.

Soviet leaders consider, as Islam considered, that the Governments of the outer world are selfish and unsound and out of touch with the people. They believe that they can offer better terms than any others to the mass of mankind. They proclaim to seven hundred and fifty million dependent people their right to be independent, and publicly and secretly they encourage revolutionary efforts to throw off the yoke of what they call Western imperialism. By intensive Spanish and Portuguese language propaganda in Latin America they prod the peoples there, upwards of one hundred million, to arise from political apathy and to take power — as Communists. Through Chinese Communists they hold out to four hundred million Chinese the promise of change from corruption and incompetence which have become traditional in some circles of Chinese officialdom. To the three hundred and fifty million of Continental Europeans, economically wrecked by two world wars, they offer a plan which, they promise, will sustain productivity more surely than an individualistic economy.

Thus the Soviet Communist Party challenges the supremacy of the so-called Christian world. Controlling at home 10 per cent of the human race, it offers leadership to a further 75 per cent, constituting the overwhelming majority of Europe,

Asia, Africa, and South America. That challenge has had an initial success. In every part of the world there are influential groups which accept leadership from Moscow.

To many, this is dismaying. It ought to dismay us to discover that the Western democracies, after ten centuries of unchallenged economic and military supremacy in the world, have so slight a spiritual hold on the masses of mankind that they eagerly listen to those who have not even shown that they can establish a good society at home. What is happening is not a measure of Soviet Communist capacity. That is still an unproved factor. What is happening is a measure of Western inadequacy. We no longer inspire confidence because we have not done that of which we are capable.

What is happening now could not have happened during the nineteenth century. Then the British Industrial Revolution, the French Revolution, with its concept of "Liberty, Equality and Fraternity," the "great American experiment" in political freedom, had created world-wide confidence in the dynamic and life-giving quality of our institutions. Now, within a few decades, that confidence is gone and our prestige is everywhere in jeopardy. The Western democracies risk being surrounded and isolated, if not overrun, by an alien faith.

What has happened is not without cause. The Western democracies have been guilty of grave lapses. As colonial powers, they should have advanced more rapidly the self-government of dependent peoples. In the American hemisphere, the United States should have been more concerned with being a good neighbor to peoples and not merely to Governments. In China, the Western democracies should have had a deeper concern than that the Chinese Government should be merely acceptable to Treaty Port traders. American industrial and labor leaders ought to have found a way so that, in the prewar depression, our economy would not have been a dead weight on the world, unable to translate idle men and idle machines into productivity.

Of course, it is easier to say that those things should have been done than to have done them. Each was a task calling for a high order of ability and statesmanship. Nevertheless, we could have done much more than we did. Some Christians saw that, but their exhortations carried little weight. So long as no foreign nation was exploiting our inadequacy it seemed safe and easier to drift along. Now that our failures are seen to be jeopardizing our society of freedom, our people may arouse themselves to remedial action. In that sense the prospect is far from dismaying.

The most important task which faces the American people is that of mental adjustment to a dynamic peace. Most of us would like a peace which is a condition of tranquillity. We would like all threat and challenge to be removed and to feel that we can safely relax. We are inclined to believe that unless we get that kind of peace, we have not peace at all. That is a dangerous mental condition. It can readily lead to a mood of frustration, for we are not likely, this time, to get a peace of tranquillity. We may, however, get something much better. Peace ought to be a condition of vigorous effort to redress wrongs and to advance the general welfare of mankind. That kind of peace is available to us. It requires no prior agreements or settlements. No nation can close to another that door of opportunity.

It is, of course, of immense importance to the life of Europe and Asia that the victors quickly agree on the terms of peace. The Conference now going on in Paris warrants the attention and effort it is receiving. On the other hand, there is no warrant for feeling that until everything is settled between the victors, nothing worth-while can be done. We should see the future in truer perspective. We should not permit ourselves to despair because of disagreements, obstacles, and delays which are now almost inevitable and which, probably for a long time, will prevent a conventional form of peace.

After long exertion the principal victors may agree on what shall be the future territorial, economic, and political status of Germans, Japanese, and Italians. However, by that time a new group of unsettlements will doubtless have risen to plague us. That will go on until a new equilibrium is established in the world as between the faith and institutions of Soviet Communism and the faith and institutions of the Western world. That equilibrium will never be achieved by paper agreements or compromises or surrenders. It will be established by the weight of facts. It must first be determined how much constructive influence each society can exert in the world. That will take time.

Such a period of unsettlement is not a disaster. It has its disadvantages and its risks. But a settled peace has, too, its risks. It is apt to generate an atmosphere of stagnation within which forces of evil readily breed. That was shown by the aftermath of World War I.

The "Big Three" of the victory of 1918 — Great Britain, France, and the United States — were all satisfied nations. Their peoples had similar beliefs and institutions. None challenged the other. All three had already achieved for themselves an advantageous position in the world. Their idea of peace was, consequently, to buttress that existing position and then to relax from the great effort of war. So they disarmed Germany and dismembered the German Empire. They broke up the Austro-Hungarian monarchy. They made the Covenant of the League and the Kellogg-Briand Pact whereby they ruled that there should be no more war. Then they went their several ways of self-enjoyment, feeling that this was safe because, internationally, everything had been settled.

For a time that peace seemed good. If this meeting were being held in the atmosphere which for a few years followed 1920, it would be easier to talk about the brotherhood of nations.

Actually, that postwar condition was unhealthy and treacherous. The Treaties of Versailles and of Trianon were not bad treaties as treaties go. The Covenant of the League and the Kellogg-Briand Pact were good as such things go. What was wrong was the spirit which dominated the principal victors. They abandoned initiative and sense of mission. That role was left to be taken over by evil spirits who brought the peace to a quick and ignominious end. The impression of the victors that all was settled proved their undoing.

History teaches that a static peace is a dangerous peace. Christ taught that same truth. Christ did not preach peace as a condition of tranquillity. Surely it was a static peace that Christ had in mind when he said, "Think not that I am come to send peace on earth: I came not to send peace, but a sword."

Christ's gospel was evolutionary, in some respects revolutionary. It taught men constantly to struggle against the imperfections of world order. So Christians want a peace that does not stifle but encourages efforts to promote human welfare.

In recent years we have been coasting on the waning momentum of the past. Now our people are beginning to see that they must choose between contributing to the world and being isolated, crowded, and jolted by the world. Once that alternative is clearly understood, there is little doubt as to what our choice will be. We shall prove again, as we have proved before, that our society of freedom can gloriously serve mankind.

Of course, a dynamic peace has its risks. It will, under present conditions, involve competition between great powers. There is always danger in such a competition. It may become so keen that the competitors will use unscrupulous methods. Each may exasperate the other to a point where ill will is great and peace can be jeopardized by minor incidents. That appears to be the greatest present danger.

Communist leaders have always professed to believe that capitalism uses war in order to keep itself going. They also profess to believe that the capitalistic nations will engage in armed conflict against Soviet Communism as the only way to overcome it. It is understandable that some phases of our nation's armament and strategic defense policies may, to Soviet leaders, seem threatening.

On the other hand, Soviet leaders themselves have never believed in tolerant methods. They have, at home, regularly employed coercion, purge, and propaganda unrelated to objective truth. They employ these same methods in aid of their foreign policy. They seem to believe that the ends which they seek justify any means.

We know, from our own political system, that it is possible to have a society which, on the one hand, is peaceful and, on the other hand, contains many different beliefs, each with devoted adherents who seek competitively to propagate their faith. However, that is possible only under a system where no one is allowed to propagate his faith by coercion, intimidation, purge, or fraud. We need, internationally, the same restraint on intolerant methods. The big question is, Will we get it?

It is possible that we can. Powerful aids are at hand to prevent the competition of great powers becoming unbridled and unscrupulous and dangerous to peace. There is no warrant whatsoever for concluding that a peace which is dynamic, competitive, and vigorous must, for that reason, culminate in violence.

First of all, none of the competitors wants war. None would willingly provoke it. Each may strain the patience of the other, but none will deliberately do what it thinks will lead to major war. The danger that exists is more a danger of miscalculation than a danger from actual malevolence. That risk of miscalculation can be reduced if the nations deal with each other in terms of candor. The cause of world peace is not really served by giving Soviet leaders the impression that the Western peoples are indifferent and complaisant toward Soviet methods of intolerance.

In the second place, we have the United Nations. Public attention focuses upon its Security Council. Actually, other aspects of the life of the United Nations may, for the present, be more important. A major purpose of the United Nations is "to be a center for harmonizing the actions of nations" in regard to economic, social, and humanitarian matters. If any member state wants to see undernourished people get more food, idle workers get more employment, ignorant people get more education, impoverished people get more economic development, dependent people get more self-government, there is an organ of the United Nations through which it can prosecute its desire.

These activities of the United Nations are already getting under way. At the first meeting of the Assembly in London, all but one of the nations holding colonial mandates expressed the intention to accept United Nations trusteeship. Great Britain is showing in India that it respects its undertaking under Chapter XI of the Charter. It is performing there a historic task of great delicacy by the use of statesmanship of a high order. The Dutch Government is promoting autonomy in the Netherlands East Indies. The United States has proposed that atomic energy should be developed by the United Nations so that there will not be competition along national lines. There already exist organs or specialized agencies to deal with food, health, economic development of backward areas, and monetary stability.

That illustrates how the United Nations can effectively serve as a harmonizing center. If the members of the United Nations will vigorously develop its humanitarian activities, that will do much to prevent human misery and discontent being exploited by particular groups for ulterior purposes. Indeed, the gain can be more than negative. The United Nations, by developing common peacetime goals, may revive the spirit of brotherhood which existed when the United Nations were fighting for common wartime goals.

Finally, there is the moral law. That is not something which only preachers talk about on Sunday. It is something that the most realistic politicians take into account. Today all national leaders talk in terms of the moral law. No doubt that reflects some hypocrisy. But the very fact that it seems necessary to present a moral façade is proof that the moral law is a recognized power.

Moral law is variously expressed and understood. Its implications do not seem to all to be the same. It needs to be translated into codified world law. But even today moral law can serve mightily to direct the conduct of nations into ways consonant with peace.

Last month the representatives of non-Roman Christian churches from fifteen lands met at Cambridge, England, to discuss the part which the churches might take in world affairs. It was unanimously agreed that "the judgment and guidance of the Christian conscience upon international problems must be clearer and more decisive than hitherto." To that end we established a permanent Commission of the Churches on International Affairs. It can be expected that that Commission will recognize that peace requires the co-operation of men of all nations, races, and creeds and that the principles upon which world order depends are those which men of good will throughout the ages have accepted as part of the moral law. A great body of Christian churches, representing many denominations and many races, is committed, as never before, to subject the conduct of nations to moral law.

Nothing that we have said affords a basis for easy optimism. We would only delude ourselves if we did not look on the future as one of peril. That, however, is no reason for pessimism. The future has always been a future of peril. Often the perils have been hidden, so that there has been no defense against them. Also, those perils brought with them no opportunity comparable to the risk. This time the perils are seen; possible defenses are at hand, and the vigorous and dynamic spirit which produces the peril can also produce an era of unprecedented progress. Thus we have great opportunity at the price of measurable risk. More than this, men should not ask.

14

Principle Versus Expediency in Foreign Policy

SHOULD our foreign policy reflect or disregard moral principles? That may sound like an academic question, but it is one of the most practical problems of our time. I chose it as my topic tonight because lawyers are a principal custodian of the belief that human conduct should conform to law and that law in turn should conform to justice. Lawyers would generally agree with Chief Justice Marshall's statement that "there are principles of abstract justice which the Creator of all things has impressed on the mind of his creature man and which are admitted to regulate, in a great degree, the rights of civilized nations."

Until recently, this point of view has dominated American foreign policy and American diplomacy.

Our Declaration of Independence was based upon an appeal to "the Laws of Nature and of Nature's God."

Our first great foreign policy, the Monroe Doctrine, was stated in terms of "asserting, as a principle" the right of the American republics to be free.

Our next great foreign policy was in relation to the Far

Address to the Missouri Bar Association, St. Louis, September 26, 1952.

East and asserted the principle of equality called "the open door."

When President Wilson called upon Congress to enter the First World War, he said "our motive" will be "only a vindication of human right," and will "prefer the interests of mankind to any narrow interest of their [our] own."

When we entered the Second World War, our purposes were set out in the Atlantic Charter. It affirmed "the right of all peoples to choose the form of government under which they will live" and "no territorial changes that do not accord with the freely expressed wishes of the peoples concerned," and it called for "the restoration of sovereign rights and self-government to those who have been forcibly deprived of them."

Of course, moral principles do not alone provide all the practical answers that men need. And no doubt, at times, our nation has strained morality to make it coincide with national self-interest. But few would doubt that the past dynamism of our nation has genuinely stemmed from a profound popular faith in such concepts as justice and righteousness and from the sense that our nation had a mission to promote these ideals by every peaceful means.

Soviet Communism reflects a view totally different from the U.S. historic view. Its creed is materialistic and atheistic. It does not admit of any moral law. Stalin mocks at the concept of eternal justice. Under the Soviet Communist system "law" is defined as the means whereby those in power impose their will on their class enemies. . . .

This creed and practice are repellent to us. Yet, within our own nation, the idea is gaining ground that our traditional American viewpoint is wrong and that, like the Russian rulers, we should discard concepts of morality, righteousness, and justice from our foreign policy-making.

Toward the close of World War II, when Soviet Russia was our cobelligerent in Europe, our Government made private agreements with Stalin which clearly violated the Atlantic Charter and the principles of international morality which it proclaimed.

It is said that we got advantages out of these agreements and that Russia would in any event have taken what she took. Probably this is so. But the significance of our action lies in the fact that our Government was willing to violate principle in order to gain what it thought were immediate practical advantages. That was nonmoral diplomacy. Of course, it was practiced in wartime, when nonmoral, short-range expediency has its maximum justification. But the same practice is being carried into some areas of our foreign policy even though that war is over. . . .

◇◇◇◇

U.S. policy toward the United Nations further illustrates the encroachment of the nonmoral approach. That story goes back to 1944, when our Government agreed with the Soviet Union on the so-called Dumbarton Oaks draft of Charter. It reflected the Soviet Communist philosophy by omitting all mention of law or justice. Primary reliance was placed on the possibility of practical deals within a Security Council dominated by the five great powers, with each having a right of veto so that it could not be bound against its will.

That plan was radically altered at the San Francisco Conference of 1945, primarily under the impact of Senator Vandenberg, whom I strongly supported in this respect. The Charter was made to provide for the development of international law, and the "principles of justice and international law" were prescribed as the guide for the settlement of disputes. The powers of the General Assembly were greatly enlarged to make it what Senator Vandenberg called "the town meeting of the world," where world opinion could be mobilized to exert an influence upon the conduct of the nations. . . .

◇◇◇◇

The American people are today disappointed in the United Nations. They made a big investment in it, an investment not only of money but, even more, of faith. The investment has not paid the expected dividends. One reason is that the United Nations is not designed to use physical force, as in Korea, and our present foreign policies are largely under the influence of those who do not believe in moral force upon which the United Nations must primarily rely. So, the United Nations has not been given a chance to work seriously on the great problems of our time.

The growing tendency toward nonmoral diplomacy is not healthy. I could give you many reasons, but I shall develop only two.

First, it inevitably makes for a break between our Government and our people. Whether we like it or not — and I like it — our people are predominantly a moral people, who believe that our nation has a great spiritual heritage to be preserved. We do not feel happy to be identified with foreign policies which run counter to what we have been taught in our churches and synagogues and in our classes on American history.

Proof of what I say is to be found in the popular reaction to the foreign policies which I have discussed.

The American people as a whole are embarrassed and

ashamed at the secret wartime agreements which we made at
the expense of our friends and allies. Some honestly feel that
what we did can be defended on the ground that in war all
moral principles go by the board. But there is little doubt but
what most of the American people feel that these agreements
are a weight upon their conscience. . . .

◇◇◇◇

As regards the United Nations, there is great popular disappointment that it has not more largely fulfilled its purpose
of promoting international law and justice, and that our policy
makers are increasingly bypassing the United Nations and
its open processes, as though our policies cannot stand the
light of day.

Of course, private diplomacy is necessary to pave the way to
the final formulation of foreign policies. But the American
people have always believed that their foreign policies should
show "a decent respect to the opinions of mankind," and they
believed that the United Nations Assembly, as the "town
meeting of the world," would assure that.

A dictatorship can, within limits, make its foreign policy
without regard to public opinion. Perhaps a more accurate
way to put it is that totalitarian dictatorships can largely create
their own domestic public opinion. Surely, however, a government like ours, which depends upon popular processes, should
conform its foreign policy in its broad outlines to what our
people can understand and approve in the light of what they
believe to be right.

A second reason against divorcing diplomacy from morality
is that this strikes at the heart of free-world unity. Today, the
United States has an inescapable responsibility for leadership.
Only leadership that inspires confidence will prevent the free

world from falling apart and being picked up, piece by piece, by Soviet Communism. United States foreign policies today represent the core of potential unity, and that core is rotten unless it is a core of moral principle. Other countries will feel, and justifiably feel, that they cannot depend upon our policies if they avowedly reflect only shifting expediencies.

Throughout the ages men have experimented with artificial means for binding nations into common action for a common cause. They have experimented with military alliances, with subsidies, with coercion. None of these methods has stood the stress and strain of fluctuating danger.

The only tie which dependably unites free peoples is awareness of common dedication to moral principles.

I have given examples of the operation of nonmoral diplomacy. There are, happily, many cases where our diplomacy has reflected moral principles. One of these, and the one with which I am most familiar, is that of the Japanese peace. There, United States initiative drew the free nations together by appealing to moral principles. Our Government invoked the spirit of forgiveness to overcome vengefulness, the spirit of magnanimity to overcome hatred, the spirit of humanity and fair play to overcome greed, the spirit of fellowship to overcome arrogance, the spirit of trust to overcome fear. The free Allied nations responded. The peace treaty became a treaty of reconciliation and liberation, and forty-nine free nations joined to sign it in a drama of peace-making unity such as the world has never seen before.

As the closing speaker in the Conference which preceded the signing, I spoke of the unity which had drawn the free nations together. I said, "What are the ties that create this unity? . . . There is a common faith, a common belief in cer-

tain great principles. . . . There can be and there will be and
there is unity as between those peoples from all corners of the
earth, from every creed, from every civilization, who do have
that common faith in great moral principles, who believe in
the worth and dignity of the human individual and who believe in justice and who believe in mercy. That is why," I said,
"we are able to agree."

Many things have changed since President Washington
delivered to the nation his Farewell Address. But we can still
usefully ponder these words: "Of all the dispositions and
habits which lead to political prosperity, religion and morality
are indispensable supports. In vain would that man claim the
tribute of patriotism who should labor to subvert these great
pillars of human happiness."

Those sentiments were uttered with primary reference to
domestic tranquillity at a time when we were but a young and
feeble nation without world-wide responsibilities. However,
what General Washington said assumes continuing and added
significance in the world of today.

There is no doubt but what our nation has quickly moved
from what seemed to be supreme security won in World War
II into what is now great danger. . . .

Some conclude that because of this peril we should cut
loose from the great principles which have historically animated our people and enabled them to guide our nation
through past perils. That is a counsel of panic. This is above
all the time to adhere loyally to those enduring principles upon
which our nation was founded. This is a time, not to change
our faith, but to renew it.

15

The Moral Foundation
of the United Nations

T HIS "Festival of Faith" is held here today because ten
years ago the United Nations was created in this city.
Also, we are assembled here because the religious people of the
world contributed largely to that great act of creation, and
they have ever since been steadfast in their support of the
United Nations. Thus, it is particularly appropriate that those
of many faiths should gather here to renew publicly their
dedication to the purposes and principles of the United
Nations.

There are many who share credit for the great accomplishment that the United Nations represents. But we can usefully
recall that moral concepts largely prompted the political decisions that, ten years ago, were recorded here.

When the Atlantic Charter was drawn up in August, 1941,
to define the hopes for a better world, it was decided to omit
reference to the creation of a world organization. It was
judged that our people did not want to repeat the League of
Nations experiment. That point of view was carried forward
into the United Nations Declaration of January 1, 1942. The

Address at the "Festival of Faith" of the San Francisco Council of Churches,
San Francisco, June 19, 1955.

religious people then came to see their responsibility and opportunity. In this country they organized and campaigned
widely to develop a public opinion favorable to world organization. The political leaders quickly responded on a bipartisan
basis.

I recall that history in order to remind ourselves that under
a representative system of government it is private persons
and organizations that must themselves make it possible to
move ahead to develop great new institutions.

Our religious people also exerted a profound influence upon
the form and character which the world organization would
take. As originally projected at Dumbarton Oaks, the organization was primarily a political device whereby the so-called great
powers were to rule the world. The projected charter did not
attempt to bind the organization to standards of justice or of
law, and the General Assembly was cast for a subordinate role.
A Security Council, dominated by five nations, each of which
had veto power, was designed to be the mainspring of the organization.

It was the religious people who took the lead in seeking
that the organization should be dedicated not merely to a
peaceful order but to a just order. It was they who sought that
reliance should be placed upon moral forces which could be
reflected in the General Assembly, the Social and Economic
Council, and the Trusteeship Council, rather than upon the
power of a few militarily strong nations operating in the Security Council without commitment to any standards of law
and justice.

The great debates of the San Francisco Conference of 1945
centered on these issues. In the end the Charter was written
so as to require the organization to conform to principles of

justice and international law. Also, the powers of the General Assembly were enlarged so that the influence of world opinion could be effectively brought to bear upon the conduct of the nations.

As we can now see, looking back, these changes were of profound significance. Indeed, without them the United Nations might not have survived these early, difficult years.

The Security Council has grievously disappointed those who believed that the great powers would act in concert to maintain world order. Not once during the ten years of its life has the UN Security Council taken direct action under the provisions of the Charter. It could not do so because the UN contingents of land, sea, and air power contemplated by the Charter have never been brought into being. Whatever the Security Council has done, as in the case of Korea, has been in the form of a recommendation, a request, or a plea — never a command. And even the scope of its recommending has been gravely limited by abuses of the so-called veto power. The political vitality of the organization has been found principally in the General Assembly and its right to recommend, a right which carries great authority because its recommendations reflect the judgment of sixty nations, representing many races, creeds, and areas.

Significant achievements have been recorded by other organs of the United Nations which are not dominated by the so-called great powers and where no veto power exists. That is particularly true of the Economic and Social Council and the Trusteeship Council. By the Declaration of Human Rights the United Nations has raised a standard which will exert a profound influence throughout the world for all future time.

So, as this past decade has unrolled, it has revealed that the power of the organization was primarily a moral power, derived from the judgment of the participating nations and their peoples as to what was right and what was wrong.

The successes of the United Nations have been largely due to those throughout the world who believe that there is a God, a divine Creator of us all; that he has prescribed moral principles which undergird this world with an ultimate authority equal to that of physical law; that this moral law is one which every man can know if only he opens his heart to what God has revealed; that these moral principles enjoin not merely love and respect of the Creator but also love and respect for fellow man, because each individual embodies some element of the Divine; and that moral principles should also govern the conduct of the nations.

It is a most encouraging fact that all governments, even including those who deny the existence of moral law, feel it necessary to try to defend their conduct, if it is challenged, in terms of moral principles. This is particularly the case when the challenge occurs, and when defense must take place, within the General Assembly. This is a testimonial to the power of moral law.

Thus, as we gather here as representatives of many faiths held throughout the world, we can find much ground for satisfaction. It has been demonstrated that the religious people of the world can generate the motive power required to vitalize a world organization by providing it with principles which are guiding not merely in theory but in fact.

We must, however, also recognize that, while the history of the United Nations shows what the religious people of the world can do, it equally discloses that they do not always do it. Sometimes they seem weak, so that moral principles do not make themselves felt. Sometimes they are confused and divided. Sometimes, also, they are intolerant and impractical, demanding solutions which do not take account of the fact that until individual human beings in sufficient numbers are themselves dedicated to high moral principles, the moral solutions which may be devised by political authorities have little effect.

To recognize these facts is to accept a challenge for the future. The first ten years of the United Nations teaches a clear lesson. The lesson is that the people of the world who are committed to the moral law have a great responsibility to assure the continued vitality of the United Nations and its capacity to influence the course of international conduct.

If the world organization were primarily operated by military power, those of us who are here would have little to do. If it were primarily operated by the self-interest of a few great powers, those of us here would have little to do. Since, however, the United Nations, as now constituted, derives its authority primarily from the moral forces generated by our respective faiths, then those who participate in this "Festival of Faith" have much to do. Indeed, we and our fellows throughout the world carry a primary responsibility.

A prophet of one of the faiths represented here said, "Not by might, nor by power, but by my Spirit, saith the Lord of hosts." That sentiment is common to all of our faiths. It can well guide us as we look to a future which contains greater hazard than any future men have ever faced, but which also contains greater opportunity. That opportunity can be grasped with confident hope if men and women of faith throughout the world develop and mobilize moral strength so that moral standards will increasingly prevail in the United Nations.

IV

The Role and Responsibility
of the Churches

Much of Mr. Dulles' thought on the issues of world order was formulated in connection with his chairmanship of the Commission of the Churches on a Just and Durable Peace, and many of his most important utterances were made to Christian audiences. But both the formal declarations and his exposition of them had in view the wider audience beyond the churches. It was the outlook and the policies of the American nation that he sought to reach and influence.

In this section are included articles and speeches in which Mr. Dulles addressed himself directly to the churches and their members and leaders, but his wider audience should not be forgotten.

It must be recalled that Mr. Dulles' activities and his leadership were not confined to the American scene. Throughout this period he was one of the most trusted and influential guides of the churches of the world, especially as they joined together in the newly formed World Council of Churches. He had presided over the meeting in Cambridge, England, in the summer of 1947, which brought into being the Commission of the Churches on International Affairs, in many respects the counterpart at the world level of the American Commission on a Just and Durable Peace; and he continued in active relationship to it as its Vice-Chairman. The following summer, in August 1948, he interrupted especially demanding public responsibilities to fly to Amsterdam to address the First Assembly of the World Council. The paper that he prepared in anticipation of the Amsterdam Assembly is perhaps the fullest exposition of the underlying presuppositions and guiding principles of all he had to say on the Christian approach to international issues, as well as a discussion of some of the most vexing problems that were then pressing.

From 1945 until he went to Washington as Secretary of State in 1953, Mr. Dulles was a member of the Board of Directors of Union Theological Seminary. He was one of the speakers at the inauguration of a new president of the seminary in November, 1945. In May, 1958, just a year before his death, he returned to the seminary for the graduation of his daughter. The address delivered on those two occasions concludes this section of selections.

16

The Church's Contribution Toward a Warless World

FOR UPWARD of thirty years I have devoted myself to international problems. Throughout most of this time I have believed that the attainment of a peaceful world order was exclusively a political problem. As I have studied more deeply I have come to realize that this is not the case. Of course proper political devices are indispensable. But such devices will not be adopted or, if adopted, will not work so long as millions of people look upon state, rather than God, as their supreme ideal.

In order to understand the reasoning which leads to my conclusion, it is necessary first to see the problem as it is presented for political solution.

I start with the very simple and fundamental premise, pointed out by Alexander Hamilton in one of his *Federalist* papers, that in every community there are men who are ambitious, fanatical, and disposed to violence. Further, as Hamilton points out, it is utopian to make political plans on the assumption that it will ever be otherwise. Given this premise,

Article in *Religion in Life*, Winter, 1940. Copyright, 1939, by Abingdon Press.

the political problem is to organize society so that such men will not dominate a community and lead it into violent and destructive ways. Fortunately, most people are normally pacific and desire to live at peace with their neighbors. The few who, out of love for adventure or lust for power or predatory instincts, tend toward violence are usually a small minority. As such, they can readily be controlled. But at times great sections of a community may come to feel that they are repressed and subjected to injustices. If so, and if they are virile and dynamic people, they then accept a leadership which offers, through force, to break through the restraints and to abolish the injustices. When this happens we have revolution. If the blame for restraint and injustice is placed upon one's own Government, we have civil war. If the responsibility is attributed to other nations, then we have international war.

Now, society has found political devices which measurably serve to protect itself from developments of this character. We set up a sort of arbiter, called government, which has a dual mandate. On the one hand, it is expected through police power to repress individual and sporadic acts of violence. On the other hand, it is expected to keep this problem within controllable limits by maintaining social conditions such that there will not develop great areas where discontent is rife and a sense of injustice is acute. This is achieved in the main by laws which are constantly being made and frequently being changed so as to provide an equality of opportunity. Even theoretical equality before the law is not sufficient. Ability is very unequal, and opportunity is largely fortuitous. It is necessary that both be controlled by law or it would lead to extreme inequalities. Thus we have laws to prevent monopoly, and laws which regulate the exploitation of property which is devoted to public service, such as railroads, utilities, etc. When there are many who are in dire need it may become necessary by taxes on income or estates to take away from some for the benefit of others. This procedure is accepted by the taxpayer, who realizes that it is better to be able to enjoy peacefully a part of what he has than to face the violent attack which would be inevitable if his Government did not function to alleviate conditions of widespread discontent.

Governments which are even moderately wise and reasonably impartial can maintain domestic order. Of course they do not always do so. We had in France, during the monarchy, and in Russia, under the czars, governments which denied the principle of equality of opportunity and which drove millions into feeling that the government functioned for the benefit of a few and without any sense of responsibility to the many who were subject to its power. The masses became so aroused as to follow leadership which was violent and ruthless, and which led them into bloody revolt. While these revolts were in sway, the outside communities were shocked and repelled at the horrors and cruelty which were incidents thereof. Today we recognize that the cause lay in the failure of political mechanism to work. It was that failure which created mass discontent which, whenever it exists, gives violent, ambitious, and unscrupulous men the opportunity to become formidable.

Through such experiences as the French and Russian Revolutions we have learned the imperative necessity of political devices which assure equality of opportunity and which constantly are at work to prevent conditions becoming rigid and fixed to the advantage of one class and to the detriment of another.

We have failed, however, to give universal application to our political knowledge. As between national groups, there exist no political mechanisms comparable to those which serve to maintain domestic tranquillity. Each state is sovereign. There is no superior arbiter to regulate the use of its powers. The rulers of each state seek primarily the advantage of their own people. This is so even though some of their powers directly and seriously affect outsiders. Toward them no responsibility is felt. For example, when the United States raises its tariff, we legislate not only upon those within the country but upon those without, who may suffer widespread distress due to the dislocation of their industries. When we prohibit or severely restrict immigration, we are not only legislating for those within the country but equally putting restraints and inhibitions upon those without. When we put difficulties in the way of foreigners investing here, we prevent them from sharing in our economic opportunities. When we arbitrarily raise the price of silver, we are not merely legislating for the benefit of silver-mine owners in the West. We are legislating a distribution of the fiscal regimes of such countries as China, which use silver for their currency. When we decide to devalue the dollar, we are legislating not only for our own people but we are breaking up currency relationships upon which depend the industry and commerce of a large part of the world.

I could continue indefinitely to illustrate how the sovereignty system violates fundamental political precepts. As we have seen, power *should* be exercised with regard for all who are subject to that power. Actually, the power of sovereignty is exercised to the end of creating for some a monopoly of advantage. No responsibility is assumed toward multitudes who are affected. Inevitably, there result areas of disaffection, which give men of violence the opportunity to make themselves formidable.

Japan, Germany, and Italy furnish modern illustrations of

the consequences of such a system.

The Japanese people are people of energy, industry, and ambition. Constituting a large population, they inhabit a small area meager in natural resources. They keenly feel the need for raw materials and for markets. But they have persistently encountered a resistance predicated largely upon the white man's conception of Japanese racial inferiority. Even in China, the Japanese found their trade blocked. England had control of the principal ports and railroads, control of the currency, and administration of the tariffs, so that from the standpoint of Japanese economic expansion in China the scale was heavily weighted against her. For many years the leadership of Japan was moderate and liberal. Under this leadership, Japan sought economic and social equality in the world. As this was denied and as the economic position in Japan became progressively more desperate, liberal leadership was ousted in favor of the army war lords who proclaimed that, by force, they would break through the restraints which the Japanese people felt had been thrown around them.

Take Italy. When World War I closed, those in Paris, like myself, who had had some occasion to study the economic and financial position of Italy, could not see how Italy would find it possible to survive. Like all the belligerents, she carried heavy burdens from the war, but unlike England, France, and the United States, she lacked the sources of food and raw materials apparently necessary to support her debt-ridden and impoverished population. It was, therefore, no surprise when grave social disturbances quickly occurred. Her liberal leaders were discarded and communism and fascism struggled for the ascendancy. Fascism won, and the Italian people followed a militant leadership which offered to make Italy powerful and to force France and England to accord Italy that share in the rich areas of North Africa which the Italian people thought had been promised them as a reward for their participation in the war.

Take Germany. It is unnecessary here to detail the severity of the treaty terms and their many departures from the pre-Armistice agreement, in reliance on which Germany had laid down her arms. Secretary of State Lansing, on the day following the delivery of the Conditions of Peace to Germany, wrote: "Resentment and bitterness, if not desperation, are bound to be the consequences of such provisions." This forecast, shared by many at the time, was quickly realized. Yet for fifteen years following the Armistice the German people followed liberal leadership under democratic institutions. But the burden continued heavy, and the sense of inequality and injustice was rendered more poignant by the economic collapse of 1930. Already then the people were beginning to listen to radical leadership which offered again to make Germany strong and to break the bounds which denied her equality of opportunity. Brüning, the last and perhaps the greatest of a series of liberal German chancellors, pleaded for treaty changes which would alleviate the condition of the German people and prevent their falling under the radical leadership of Hitler and the Nazi Party. His pleadings were in vain, and the German people finally accepted the leadership and control of the proponents of force.

I do not recite the history of Japan, Italy, and Germany with a view to placing personal blame on the leaders of England, France, or the United States. They had a power, in respect of such matters as trade, control of raw materials, markets, and money, which vitally affected the peoples of Japan, Italy, and Germany. They exercised that power without responsibility for the welfare of these other peoples. In so doing, they lived up to the dictates of the sovereignty system.

But if I do not blame these rulers, neither do I place blame upon the Japanese, German, and Italian people. They are in the main orderly and peace-loving, quite the equals in this respect of the Americans, English, and French. But like any dynamic and virile people, when they fall into economic distress, they rebel against restraints and humiliations ascribable to other states and, like all revolutionists, they then follow leadership which extols violence.

The fault is that of the system. That which has occurred was bound to have occurred. And such occurrences are bound to repeat themselves under any international system which ignores this political axiom: there are always, in every country and at every time, those who are eager to lead the masses in ways of violence. They can be rendered innocuous only by preventing the many from feeling that they are subject to power which is exercised without regard for their welfare and which condemns them to inequalities and indignities.

Now, the failure to apply in the international field the lessons we have learned in the national field is not because the problem is essentially different or inherently unsolvable. Various solutions are known which offer good chance of success. These solutions generally assume one of two forms, which may conveniently be described as the "league" formula and the "federal" formula. The League of Nations is, of course, the outstanding example of an attempted solution of the first type. Under the League Covenant, the nations bound themselves to two essential principles. Article 19 of the League Covenant empowered the Assembly of the League from time to time to "advise the reconsideration by Members of the League of treaties which have become inapplicable and the consideration of international conditions whose continuance might endanger the peace of the world." Article 16 provided that in the event that any member resorted to war without first submitting the dispute to arbitration or the Council it would be subject to nonintercourse measures applied by the other League members. There was thus present in the League, in theory at least, the two elements indispensable to the preservation of peace. There was, first, the obligation to make changes from time to time necessary to prevent that mass discontent which always turns to dynamic leadership and makes it formidable. Second, there was provided collective power sufficient to repress violence which, so long as it is not backed by a great popular movement, is sporadic and controllable.

Actually, the League failed because at no time were the dominant members of the League ever ready to give vitality to Article 19, and to revise treaties or to alleviate conditions which obviously threatened the peace of the world. But in principle the conception was sound.

There are, of course, many possible variations of the political formula represented by the League, notably those which call for regional leagues which bind together those states whose powers are particularly apt to be overlapping in their scope.

The second line of political approach is that represented by the federal system. The federal system recognizes that sovereignty is a bundle of powers which do not necessarily all have to be vested in the same entity or exercised with regard for the same group of people. Certain powers, for example those relating to trade, immigration, and money, operate upon a far wider circle of persons than do those relating to sanitation, education, etc. It, therefore, vests the first set of powers in a body having responsibility toward a large group of people, while it leaves the second group of powers in bodies responsible only to smaller groups of persons. Our own Constitution is, of course, the best-known example of the federal system, but the federal principle is subject to indefinite expansion and has many possible variations. For instance, any number of states might agree that the matter of trade between them was a matter of common concern and, therefore, that authority over trade between these nations should be vested in a body which derived its authority from and had responsibility toward all the peoples concerned. In this way power and responsibility tend to become coextensive, and we do away with a condition whereby certain persons are restrained and restricted by power exercised without regard for their welfare.

I have no intention here to advocate any particular political formula. I merely want to make clear that there *are* possible solutions and that there is no reason why we cannot find, for the international field, political devices comparable to those which serve in the national field to prevent that mass discontent which makes quick transition to mass violence.

At the Conference at Geneva, which I attended last summer on the initiative of the World Council of Churches, there were formulated certain principles which, it was said, "stand out as clear applications of the Christian message." The first of these was that political power and responsibility should be coextensive. The second was that power should be exercised in accordance with the principle that all human beings are of equal worth in the eyes of God and should be so treated in the political sphere. A third principle was that it is as necessary to effect changes in the interest of justice as to secure the protection of the *status quo*.

These are not merely Christian principles. They are the principles which must be applied within any society which effectively maintains domestic tranquillity. They are principles which can be extended into the international field through mechanisms such as those I have mentioned. But, and this is of the essence, *any* such formula involves some dilution of sovereignty. For example, under the league system a member state may be called upon to contribute to change conditions elsewhere, the continuance of which might endanger the peace of the world. If, for instance, the League had functioned and the United States were a member thereof, we might have been called upon to take a different attitude toward Japanese immigration and toward Japanese goods from that which, purely in our own interests, we had decided to take. It might have been felt that thereby mass discontent within Japan might have been alleviated, moderate leadership preserved, and explosion into China prevented. Now, any nation which honestly agrees, in advance, to contribute to changes deemed necessary to preserve the peace elsewhere has deprived itself of some of the panoply of full sovereignty. Similarly, under the federal system, power is divided up as between different bodies having different jurisdictions. There is no single entity which has the majesty of full power. Thus the establishment of a common money might be vested in a body created by and responsible to the English, French, German, and American people. This would deprive our own Government of exclusive control over a national money and we could not, for example, repeat our 1933 attempt to cure our depression by devaluing our particular money. Any peoples which participate in a league system or a federal system inevitably deprive their national government of certain attributes of power.

It is at this point that we encounter the serious and presently insuperable obstacle. It is an obstacle for which the church must accept large responsibility. It is an obstacle which, perhaps, the church alone can dispel. It is this: to great masses of mankind their personified state is, in effect, their god; it represents the supreme object of their devotion; its power and dominion are, to them, sacred, and to subtract therefrom is akin to sacrilege.

It is apparent that so long as this sentiment prevails it is impossible for a sound international order to be established, for any such order requires a dilution of sovereignty as now practiced.

One hundred and thirty-five years ago, in New England, a group of Christians comprising the Massachusetts Peace Society appointed a committee to study the causes and results of war. They found among other causes what they referred to as an "infatuation" and "delusion" by which individuals identify themselves with the nation to which they belong and invest this personified entity with godlike attributes such that its majesty becomes of primary importance. With respect to this cause of war they said: "Should the increase of moral light in the ages to come be in the ratio of that in the past, we predict that this sentiment will be regarded by posterity as one of the most childish and absurd of the present age."

Unhappily, it would appear that moral light has not increased in the ratio expected by the Massachusetts Peace Society. A delusion which they expected would be quickly dissipated has on the contrary grown until today it is the most powerful and dangerous force in the world. It is today the formidable obstacle which makes it impossible to apply in the international field those political solutions which work within the domestic field.

How do we account for the fact that this delusion has engrafted itself so firmly upon us? The explanation, I think, lies in the failure of the churches to provide mankind with a loftier means of satisfying its spiritual cravings. Most men are aware of their own finite character and their own inadequacies. They seek to identify themselves with some external being which appears more noble and more enduring than are they themselves. Most men are not purely selfish. They are attracted to a cause which is so sure of itself that it dares to call for sacrifice. Mankind demands a creed through which to achieve spiritual exaltation. This creed *should* be a religious one. But it is not. Our religious leaders have seemed unable to make vital and gripping the concept of God as revealed by Christ. Has the church, in recent years, called for sacrifices even remotely approaching those called for in the name of patriotism? Religion does not become more vital as it becomes softer and easier. On the contrary, the people lose confidence in a creed, the exponents of which dare not call for sacrifice on its behalf.

It is because of this failure that the false gods of nationalism have been imagined to fill the spiritual need which most men feel.

The present situation is a cause of deep concern to those who genuinely seek a system of world order. Many political leaders, it is true, give only lip service to this concept. To most of them it is a smug formula for advancing the national interest. But there exists in every country an influential group of men who understand the political problem and earnestly and intelligently seek its solution. But, under present conditions, they are impotent. Any sound world order can be achieved only by a major operation upon sovereignty. But you cannot operate upon an entity which is popularly deified.

I have been deeply impressed by the fact that when, as at Oxford three years ago and in Geneva this year, there met together Christians of conflicting nationalities none of the difficulties between their nations seemed insuperable. They quickly fell into the category of those matters which are calmly discussed and peacefully settled. This is because under such circumstances the problems are discussed purely from the standpoint of the welfare of the human beings involved. What aggravates such problems beyond the possibility of solution is their presentation, not in terms of the welfare of human beings, but in terms of the relative powers and prerogatives of personified nations each of which, by its own people, is looked upon as quasi god.

Can the church repair its failure? That I do not know. I am discouraged when I see Christian leaders, in countries which include our own, seeking to identify righteousness with one or another national cause. In many churches the national flag and national anthem today replace the Christian symbols. This seems the easy way. Thereby an anemic church draws vitality from the coursing blood of nationalism. But this not merely aggravates the problem we are seeking to solve. It also exposes a dependence of the churches upon the human rather than the divine. Political leaders are not slow to draw the obvious inference. The church becomes to them a human institution upon which they can stamp whenever it serves their purpose. This today is occurring in not a few of the so-called Christian countries.

The other way is the evangelical way. It requires that we vitalize belief in a God who is the Father of us all, a God so universal that belief in him cannot be reconciled with the deification of nation. This seems a hard, slow way. But it is the way Christ showed. He did not engage in political controversy and had little to say about the functioning of state or even of war and peace. He issued one solemn guide and warning, namely, that we should not render unto Caesar that which is God's. We have come to our present pass because that warning has gone unheeded. All that is best and noblest in mankind has been put at the service of a political mechanism which is human and fallible and which, in its international operation, violates every Christian precept. We have been rendering unto Caesar a spiritual devotion and a sacrifice which belong only unto God. Thereby we have encompassed our own destruction.

There can be no salvation until we have set right the fundamentals. The urgent task of the church is to restore God as the object of human veneration and to recreate in man a sense of duty to fellow man. National governments must be seen to be what they are — pieces of political mechanism which involve no sanctity and which must be constantly remolded and adapted to meet the needs of a world which is a living, and therefore a changing, organism.

I know that it is difficult to transfer devotion to that which is abstract and universal. I know that it is difficult to enlist sacrifice except by invoking the ideology of combat and of hate. But I also know that mankind is paying a fearful price for its worship of false gods and that never before did the world so need a vital belief in a universal God. That need is the measure of our opportunity and it must equally be the measure of our works and of our faith.

17

Christian Responsibility for Peace

THE CHRISTIAN churches of this country bear a heavy responsibility for peace. If there should be war between the United States and Russia, it might be due to circumstances beyond our control. More probably, the war would be one which the churches could have prevented. If we should fail in that prevention, it would not be through lack of desire, for the churches' desire for peace is immense; it would not be for lack of power, for if the churches work zealously and in unison, their power too is immense. If there is failure, it would be because our churches do not have the know-how. That is the elusive, often lacking, quality.

I doubt that the churches can prevent war merely by preaching the evil of war. Also, I doubt that the churches can prevent war by attempting to prescribe in detail the conduct of foreign affairs. I do think it likely that war can be prevented if our churches assure that our people will not, in the words of the psalmist, "rage and imagine vain things." In other words, if our people are free of hatred and anger

---

Address at the General Conference of The Methodist Church, Boston, May 4, 1948.

so that they think straight and see truly, war probably will be avoided.

There is, as I say, a chance that war might come about through Russian action which we could not prevent. But the available evidence and the logic of the situation strongly indicate that Russian leaders do not now want war and would not initiate war unless they genuinely felt that war was our intention. The Russian nation has already achieved its traditional ambitions in the Far East and in the West. Only toward the Middle East are there unsatisfied national ambitions which war might realize.

On the other hand, Russia suffered horribly from the last war. Because she emerged victorious and because her leaders now adopt a hard attitude, we forget how deeply she was wounded. Scarcely a beginning has yet been made in healing those wounds, and the Russian people who survived the last war profoundly dread any repetition.

So, while there is a risk of war on Russian initiative, which our national policy must take into account, it seems that that risk is small if we conduct ourselves properly.

From the standpoint of the United States, there is no reason whatever for war against Russia. We have no quarrel with the Russian nation, which has nothing that we want, and there is a tradition of unbroken friendship between our peoples.

The danger of war comes from the fact that the Soviet Communist Party is attacking free institutions by methods of penetration, propaganda, and terrorism which the American people deeply resent and which create in them a disposition to strike back. That frame of mind leads to thoughts of war because the world has for centuries been highly organized on a national basis; international controversies have been those of state against state, and war has been the accepted instrument of solution. Also, the conventional defense against aggression is military defense and deeply rooted habits of thought and action lead our people now to turn to that. Also, there is a vested interest in that type of defense, in building it up and, perhaps, in using it.

The instinctive reaction of our people, while understandable, is unfortunate because it does not fit the present case. We are not witnessing a conventional type of effort by one state to take something away from another state. It is not a state, but it is a party, which originates that which arouses our people. It is not operating against us as a nation but against our institutions. What is happening is novel, the like of which men have not seen since, one thousand years ago, the new and dynamic Moslem faith struck out against the established institutions of Christendom. Islam, however, invoked military effort to make its faith prevail, and there is little evidence that the Soviet Communist Party now has that intention. It does believe in violence, coercion, and terrorism, but as weapons against individuals. War is not its preferred method. Also, war is not an appropriate countermeasure to the Communist Party attack. In fact, instead of defending our free institutions, war would weaken them, and in the long run probably inure greatly to the benefit of the Communist Party. That party's first great opportunity came out of World War I. Its second great opportunity came out of World War II, and a third world war might well make the Communist Party supreme in the world.

It is possible to pile argument upon argument to show that war is unnecessary and could not serve its intended purpose. The problem of preserving peace is, however, not at the moment a problem of marshaling arguments. It is a problem of finding minds that are receptive to reason. We are seeing in this country a natural tendency to rush to arms in time of peril. That tendency is accentuated by a mood of hatred, which makes some want to lash out blindly. Many also feel that war is inevitable and that it is better to get it over with, particularly when we still have atomic bombs and the Russians do not. Also, the thought of war no longer evokes the horror which prevailed when atomic bombs ended World War II. The result is an inflammable situation which could be exploded by even a minor incident.

The immediate task is to create an atmosphere such that the future will be determined by reason, not by accident.

That is a task which peculiarly falls within the province of our churches. We have free institutions because our founders took a Christian view of the nature of man. They believed that men were endowed by their Creator with certain inalienable rights and also that men had a duty to God and fellow man which would induce the self-control needed to make freedom socially tolerable. Those two interdependent religious conceptions are the foundation of our free society.

There is no doubt that a free society has its dangers. There is always danger that the people will be swept by mass emotionalism into doing reckless and unreasonable things. That risk is one which Soviet leaders constantly harp upon to justify their system of dictatorship and their control of press and speech. A free society justifies itself only if its members exercise self-control. If our churches will see to that, they will make a great contribution to peace. . . .

◇◇◇◇

It would be much more exciting if church leaders could invent some dramatic, specific formula which of itself would resolve the tensions which now exist. Perhaps that can happen. I hope so. But peace is more apt to come about through a gradual day-to-day improvement of the situation. If the churches will realize this, they will, I am sure, exert their influence in favor of the myriad of little acts which, in the aggregate, exert a tremendous influence. Little things multiplied many times become great things. If the American people will individually exercise the self-control and self-restraint which is the duty of members of a free society, then the situation will instantly improve because then reason and calm counsel can prevail. There are plenty of reasons available, and there is plenty of calm leadership. But, in times of crisis, reason and calm leadership become impotent unless the people themselves exercise self-control. To assure that is the first and imminent task. If the churches will do it, they will have made an indispensable contribution to peace.

To restore clear vision and calm thinking will not, of itself, produce peace, but only the conditions that make peace possible. Some think that peace can be assured if we see only the good that is in others and the evil that is in ourselves. I believe that that involves blurred vision rather than clear vision, and that peace requires our seeing clearly what there is of righteousness in our institutions and then defending that, not with arms, but with faith. War is always likely when a people largely endowed with worldly goods do not have faith in their institutions and practices. That situation invites attack, and those who are not armed with faith are apt to be quick on the trigger.

Arnold Toynbee in his volume *Civilization on Trial* refers to the fact that Western civilization has "been living on spiritual capital, I mean clinging to Christian practice without possessing the Christian belief – and practice unsupported by belief is a wasting asset, as we have suddenly discovered, to our dismay, in this generation."

Our people still have Christian faith to a degree equal to the past; at least that is indicated by statistics. Our national practices still produce bountifully. But the connection between faith and practice seems broken, and that is a source of weakness and danger. It is time either to get new institutions in which we can place confidence and take pride or to recapture our faith in our existing institutions.

Our churches have, perhaps, contributed to breaking the connection between our faith and our practices by emphasizing the imperfection of what is. What is, is always imperfect, and it is clearly the duty of the churches to point that out and to urge Christian citizens to seek constant improvement. It would be morally indefensible and practically disastrous to identify what is with perfection and to attempt to sustain it unchanged. But that attitude does not involve discrediting what is the essence of our political institutions — that is the procedure by which change is made.

The quality in our institutions which justifies our confidence is that they make possible change which is peaceful and which accords with the view of the majority without doing violence to the minority. In that respect our institutions reflect a Christian concept of the nature of man and of the dignity and worth of the human personality. It is, above all, that method of change which distinguishes our society from many others, notably that of Soviet Communism. . . .

◇◇◇◇

Soviet professions attract great attention and a considerable following for the very reason that the Soviet Party is dedicated to carrying them out by methods of violence. When people are so sure they are right that they are willing to die and kill for their views, that seems to carry great conviction. Fanaticism gives an impression of zeal which is lacking when people seek their goals by peaceful means. But Christians, just as they reject war as a method of achieving international goals, must equally reject coercion and violence against the individual as a method of achieving social goals. Such methods are unchristian, and whenever they are invoked — even in support of Christianity, as has happened — the result is an evil and ugly thing.

I believe that Christians can proudly recognize the worth of institutions which, because they reflect a Christian conception of the nature of man, provide for change in ways that respect the dignity and worth of the human person. Certainly our institutions are not perfect. But it is undeniable that they have been the means whereby there has been steady progress toward Christian goals. Those goals are not nearly achieved. There is much to be done, particularly in terms of broad social welfare. The churches ought never to relax their pressure for constant improvement, and Christians ought always to be humble in the face of present inadequacies. But by demonstrating their capacity for peaceful change, our free institutions have, I submit, earned the faith and confidence of our people.

Let us not fear that faith. It will not lead to war, either a national war or a "holy war." Faith in things, interest that is vested — that is what is dangerous and stultifying. But faith in institutions which on the one hand facilitate change and on the other hand assure that it will occur peacefully, without violating human personalities — that is something very different. Such a faith, if coupled with works, is the best possible insurance against assault from without. Also, that faith will assure against our own resort to arms. We shall have new confidence in the rightness and in the efficacy of peaceful ways. As we believe in them nationally, so, internationally, we shall seek peaceful processes and those habits of tolerance which permit different faiths to subsist peacefully side by side.

That is our goal; may God guide us to it.

18

*The Christian Citizen
in a Changing World*

THIS PAPER is written by a layman who has been active
in the field of international affairs. It is primarily an action
paper, not a theological paper. It accepts, explicitly or im-
plicitly, basic Christian beliefs and suggests how, in the actual
situation, they may impose on Christian citizens a duty of
practical conduct.

There is no thought that the church should endorse the
conclusions reached or the lines of action suggested. The
writer is, indeed, one who believes that the church ought not
to make authoritative pronouncements with respect to detailed action in political, economic, or social fields. Practical
political action is not often a subject for authoritative moral
judgments of universal scope. Those who act in the political
field must deal with the possible, not with the ideal; they must
try to get the relatively good, the lesser evil; they cannot,
without frustration, reject whatever is not wholly good; they
cannot be satisfied with proclaimed ends, but must deal with
actual means. Those necessities prevail conspicuously in the

A paper written as part of the preparation for the First Assembly of the
World Council of Churches, Amsterdam, August, 1948. Printed in full in
The Church and the International Disorder (Harper & Brothers, 1948).

international field where tradition, national interest and group loyalty have accumulated to an unusual degree. They place limits on what is practically possible; they introduce error into every human judgment; they increase the ever-present risk that men will see as "right" that which is self-serving.

Facts such as those mentioned require that the churches should exercise great caution in dealing with international political matters. They should not seem to put the seal of God's approval upon that which at best may be expedient, but which cannot wholly reflect God's will.

It does not, however, follow that Christian faith and Christian political action are unrelated. All citizens have to act in relation to political matters — inaction being only a form of action, a clearing of the way for others who do act. Also, Christian citizens, when they act, will try to be guided by Christian insight and Christian inspiration. Political institutions molded by those who take a Christian view of the nature of man will be different from those molded by atheists. What the churches elect to say will have political consequences. What they elect to keep silent about will also have political consequences. So the churches, too, have a relationship to practical politics that is inescapable.

Since that is so, it seems that the churches ought to know what are the problems which Christian citizens face. "Thy word is a lamp unto my feet, and a light unto my path." But the churches cannot throw light of the Word upon the Christians' paths unless they know where those paths lie and what are the obstacles that need to be illumined lest the Christian pilgrim stumble and fall. It is useful, no doubt, for Christian citizens to be inspired by the vision of a distant, heavenly scene. But also it is useful to have light upon the way.

Obviously, Christian citizens throughout the world do not

all face identical problems or have identical duties. No single presentation can adequately inform the churches. There are, in the world, many paths for Christians, all leading toward a central point, the doing of God's will on earth. Some paths lead from the East, some from the West, some from the North, some from the South. Each of these paths has obstacles of its own. In turn, these obstacles constantly shift. What is described now may be irrelevant by tomorrow. Despite the fact that the scene is world-wide and shifting, the churches should seek to keep informed. Otherwise, they cannot keep each way illuminated with shafts of the divine light.

This paper seeks to show in relation to international affairs, what is the political path which some Christians have to tread, what they see as the obstacles ahead, and how they think they can, perhaps, overcome these obstacles and wrest the initiative from forces of evil, ignorance, and despair, which exist in every land and which seem to be conspiring to overwhelm mankind with awful disaster.

The writer recognizes, quite frankly, that the path he describes is a path which leads from the West. He knows full well that that way differs from other ways. These, too, should be known, for the church concedes no priority or privilege to any nation, race, or class.

As the churches come to know better the practical problems which Christian citizens have to face and the lines of action in which they may become engaged, the churches in turn will be better able to minister to the actual needs. They will be better able to show, to each and to all, that Christ is indeed the Way, the Truth, and the Life. As Christ is so revealed, he will draw all men unto him, and that supreme loyalty will provide the unifying force which otherwise men seek in vain.

THE INEVITABILITY OF CHANGE

The basic political and social fact that citizens must face up to is the fact of change. Life and change are inseparable. Human beings constantly change. So, too, do human societies. There are always some who unthinkingly wish that they could stop change and freeze a moment into eternity. That cannot be and, indeed, we should not want it to be. If it happened, it would mean an end and the replacement of life with death.

Christians do not regret the inevitability of change. Rather, they see in it a cause for rejoicing. Some religions see man as bound to a wheel which turns and on the turning of which he can exert no influence. As a result of that assumption it follows, for them, that the ideal mental state is one of indifference and renunciation of hopes and efforts which can end only in frustration. The Christian believes that he can do something about change to determine its character and, accordingly, he looks upon the inevitability of change as something that provides opportunity. That opportunity has a dual aspect. Outwardly, there is the opportunity to make the world more nearly one in which God's will is done on earth as it is in heaven. Inwardly, there is the opportunity for personal growth and development which comes out of grappling with situations and trying to mold them.

When there is change, something that *is* disappears and something that *was not* appears. Also, whenever there is change there is a means, a force, that brings change to pass. The Christian seeks the disappearance of that which he deems imperfect. But the disappearance of something imperfect is not, of itself, sufficient to make change good. If that were so, all change by whatever means would be good, for everything is to some extent imperfect, and there cannot be change without the disappearance of some imperfection. The Christian tries to appraise change not merely in terms of what disappears but also in terms of what replaces that which disappears. This appraisal involves an appraisal of means as well as ends, for the means by which change is accomplished makes an indelible impression upon the result and becomes, indeed, a part of the result.

For Christians, the great social task is to deal with the forces that make *some* change imperative so that (*a*) these forces will make their principal impact on what can be and will be replaced by something better; (*b*) the forces for change will leave relatively immune what at the moment cannot be replaced by something better; and (*c*) the forces for change will not themselves be evil and unchristian in character.

THERE IS NEED THAT CHANGE BE INSTITUTIONALIZED

Political leaders who have or want power usually talk much alike as to the social ends they seek. They all propose to increase the sum total of human happiness. The manifestos of communism, nazism, and democracy have much in common. Many people pick their leaders simply on the basis of their promises and on the basis of the zeal which they seem to manifest. Sometimes the very violence with which leaders would seek their ends seems a recommendation, as being a proof of zeal.

The Christian citizens will consider not only the social ends which are professed in words but also those elements which, we have seen, make up the nature of change. They will inquire into whether the changes proposed will replace something imperfect by something better, will leave immune what cannot be improved, and will avoid means which are evil. They have learned that the actual result will probably be determined more by the means than by the professions of long-range ends. Also, they know that a choice of violent means may not indicate honest zeal but a lust for the increased power which comes to political leaders whenever violent means are sanctioned.

Difference of opinion about means is often the critical difference. Christians prefer means of the kind which, they believe, Christ taught. They are not inclined to look with approval upon means of violence and coercion. They have seen that over the ages war, revolution, and terrorism have been repeatedly invoked for noble ends. But change brought about in that way is hurried and it usually gets out of control. It crushes blindly what happens to lie in its path. At times it inspires fine and sacrificial qualities, but also it develops in men hatred of fellow man, vengefulness, hypocrisy, cruelty, and disregard of truth. History seems to show that, when these evil qualities are invoked to produce good ends, in fact they vitiate or postpone the professed ends. Change sought by methods of force, violence, and coercion seldom produces lasting, good results.

The Oxford Conference of 1937 said:
"Wars, the occasions of war, and all situations which conceal the fact of conflict under the guise of outward peace, are marks of a world to which the church is charged to proclaim the gospel of redemption. War involves compulsory enmity, diabolical outrage against human personality, and a wanton distortion of the truth. War is a particular demonstration of the power of sin in this world and a defiance of the righteousness of God as revealed in Jesus Christ and him crucified. No

justification of war must be allowed to conceal or minimize this fact."

Some Christians believe that the use of violence is of itself so unchristian that it should never under any circumstances be resorted to. Most Christian citizens, it seems, do not accept that view. The vast majority appear to believe that, while they ought not themselves to initiate the use of force as a means, once force is invoked by others to do injustice, and to impose conditions violative of the moral law and of the Christian conception of the nature of man, then to use force to prevent those results may be the lesser of two evils. Christians would generally agree that methods of change other than violence are to be preferred because violence, unless it be the dispassionate force of police power under law, almost always generates unchristian qualities which cancel out, or at least greatly dilute, the value of the changes which violence brings about.

If force is discarded as the accepted means of change, then there have to be established procedures and political organizations for the purpose of making peaceful change. Such procedures have to a considerable extent been established within states, but they are lacking in the international field. There, as elsewhere, history teaches the inevitability of change. If one examines a historical atlas and looks at the political arrangement of the world one hundred years ago, two hundred years ago, and so forth, one cannot but be impressed by the magnitude of the changes that have occurred. Most of these changes have been effected by war or the threat of war. Each war brought about the disappearance of something that was imperfect. Often it involved the doing away of power in some men and nations which had become disproportionate to their ability or readiness to use that power for the general welfare.

In that sense, the change was good. But, also, the method of violence has done terrible things to the hearts of men. It has not brought individuals to greater love of God and neighbor in accordance with the great commandments. Indeed, the result has been, on the whole, quite the contrary. The prestige of Christianity in the world has been gravely impaired by the frequency with which the so-called Christian nations have used violence as a method of international change. Furthermore, the hatred, falsification, cruelty, and injustice incident to each war have, we can see in retrospect, done much to provoke new war and all the evil that that entails.

INSTITUTIONS FOR CHANGE REQUIRE DECIDING WHO CONTROLS

Christian citizens can readily conclude, as a generalization, that there ought to be political institutions which will enable international change to take place in a peaceful way. But that conclusion is not, of itself, very significant. It cannot have any practical consequence unless also there is another decision, namely, whose judgment will determine the timing and the nature of peaceful change. Change *ought* to be based upon reflection and deliberate choice, not upon accident and force. Of course. But *whose* reflection and choice are to be controlling? That is a hard question. Within nations there is no uniform answer. In the international field few have attempted seriously to answer it, and those few are not in agreement. Uncertainty, disagreement, and competition about that largely explain why, in the international field, change has so far been left mostly to accident and violence.

It used to be widely held that political decisions should be made by rulers who were not responsible to their people.

Today, it is generally agreed, at least in theory, that it is better that men should be self-governing through some representative process which they control. But that theory is seldom carried out in practice, even within nations. In many countries of the world, power is exercised by dictators. Of these, there are many types. Some are men who, loving power, have taken it and make no attempt to rationalize their action. Often, by written constitution, their government is a "republic" or "democracy." Some dictators are benevolent, taking power only to tide over a real or imagined crisis. Some exercise dictatorial power in order, professedly, to train the masses and discipline them into a common mold which, it is thought, ought to precede self-government. Such purposeful dictatorships are often termed "totalitarian."

There are other countries where the peoples do in fact, through representative processes, exercise a very large measure of influence upon the choices that are made as to change. These societies customarily describe themselves as "free societies." Some call them "responsible societies" or "self-disciplined societies." We use the phrase "free societies" because it has wider popular use, although we recognize and hereafter emphasize that there is interdependence between freedom and self-discipline and sense of responsibility. We also recognize that even in the so-called free societies there are usually some who are, in fact, excluded from equal opportunity to participate in the deliberative process which determines when and how change shall be effected.

In no country is there a pure democracy in the sense that all of the people have equal and direct participation in all of the deliberations which determine change. Also, in no country are dictatorships so absolute that those who possess the governmental power wholly disregard what they sense to be the wishes of the people. Even so, the organization of the different nations shows that there are great and momentous differences, both in theory and in practice, as to whose choice should determine change. These differences are a great obstacle to institutionalizing change at the international level. Therefore, the matter deserves further consideration.

FORMS OF GOVERNMENT COMPATIBLE WITH CHRISTIAN IDEALS

Christians tend to favor the free society of self-discipline. That is probably because Christians think of man primarily in terms of the individual and his relations to God and to fellow man. It is only individuals who have souls to be saved, and God, it seems, is not concerned with nations, races, and classes, *as such*. He is concerned with individual human beings. Christians, who believe that, want a political society which, recognizing the value and the sacredness of individual personality, gives the individual the opportunity to develop in accordance with the dictates of his own conscience and reason, and also puts on him a responsibility to exercise freedom with regard for the welfare of fellow men.

Christians believe that for one man to possess arbitrary power over his fellow men is an unchristian relationship. It usually corrupts him who rules and it tends to debase those who are ruled, if in fact they acquiesce in being ruled.

Furthermore, Christians believe that civil laws made by men should, so far as possible, reflect the moral law. We believe that there is implanted in every individual a potential awareness of right and wrong and that under favoring conditions the composite of such individual judgments will reflect the moral law better than the judgments of absolute and self-perpetuating rulers. Also, as a practical matter, unless laws reflect and codify the moral judgments of those subject to them, they are not apt for long to be enforceable.

For such reasons, Christians tend to prefer the free society. But also they recognize that peaceful and selective change is not assured merely by giving people a right of suffrage. The voice of the people is not always the voice of God. It is easy to arouse masses for destruction without regard to the problem of replacement. Mob psychology is seldom conducive to selective change, and it does not in fact represent individual reflection and choice.

A free society, if it is to effect peaceful and selective change, must be a society where in addition to the right to vote the people possess and use personal freedoms and access to information and the opportunity to exchange and propagate thoughts and beliefs so that there is, on an individual basis, genuine reflection and sober choice of minds and spirits which are both free and developed by use and self-discipline. There is also need of tolerance, particularly in the sense that political power may not be used to promote any particular creed.

The free society may at times of emergency, such as the emergency created by war, grant one man or a few men very extraordinary, even dictatorial, powers. But the people will reserve effectively the opportunity to end these powers when the occasion for them has passed.

Economically, a free society does not have to be a laissez-faire society. There are some who profess to believe that only a laissez-faire society adequately encourages individual development. There are, however, few who today would put that belief wholly into practice. In all states, even those most dedicated to free enterprise, there is governmental control of at least some of the tools of production, such as railroads and public utilities, which are endowed with a special public interest. In most countries, there are important collective and co-operative enterprises. It would seem that there is no inherent incompatibility between the Christian view of the nature of man and the practice of economic communism or state socialism. Communism in the sense of "from each according to his abilities, to each according to his needs," was early Christian practice.

In the modern world, particularly where there is industrialization, there is much interdependence and necessity for co-operation. In part, this necessity can be met by individual knowledge of how, in a complicated society, individual acts affect others. To that knowledge there needs to be added self-control and sense of duty to fellow man so that individuals will voluntarily refrain from acts which they see have injurious consequences more than offsetting the benefits to self. But even where the people are possessed of much self-control and sense of duty there may have to be added public controls and centralized direction to promote the equitable distribution of goods in short supply and to ensure co-operative and co-ordinated action on a scale adequate to the needs of our complicated economics.

One may have different judgments as to what economic structure is best adapted to modern conditions and as to the kind of incentive which is required to insure needed productivity. There are times and conditions when the most effective appeal is to self-interest. There are other times and conditions when the greatest appeal may be to men's sacrificial spirit. The Christian church seeks constantly to make men's motives more lofty and to invoke concern for others rather than for self. Christians believe that those that are strong ought to bear the infirmities of the weak, and not to please themselves. But there are few who fully heed that injunction. Christian citizens in seeking to organize society have to take account of what men *are*, not what the church thinks they ought to be.

From the Christian viewpoint, the essential is political and economic conditions which will help, and not stifle, growth by the individual in wisdom and stature and in favor with God and man. We want conditions which in so far as practical will, in fact, exalt the dignity of man. The essential in this respect is the content, not the form. The conditions which best assure that will doubtless vary from time to time and from place to place.

It is not possible to attach the Christian label to any particular political or economic organization or system to the exclusion of all others. It is not possible to say that free enterprise is Christian and socialism unchristian — or vice versa. It is not possible to say that a popular representative system of government is Christian, or temporary dictatorship inherently unchristian. It is, however, possible to condemn as unchristian societies which are organized in disregard of the Christian view of the nature of man. This would include those which are totalitarian in the sense that they recognize the right of some men to seek to bring the thoughts, beliefs, and practices of others into conformity with their will, by processes of coercion.

It could be argued that if Christians really believe that the truth is uniquely revealed by God through Jesus Christ, they ought to seek an organization of the state which would make it possible to use every power, including police power, to compel acceptance of that truth and the liquidation of heretics and nonconformers.

There have been times when that viewpoint prevailed.

Christianity over its two thousand years has had many experiences and has learned much. It has learned that when Christians use political power, or any coercive or artificial means, to give special advantage to their distinctive sect, the outcome is apt to be an ugly thing. We reject methods which, history seems to teach, pervert Christianity. If we reject totalitarianism for ourselves, we a fortiori reject it for others. Believing that our own faith cannot remain pure when coupled with methods of intolerance, we also believe that no faith can enter into that partnership without corruption.

PEACEFUL CHANGE IS POSSIBLE

Practical experience seems to show that where the people have a considerable degree of self-discipline, where they recognize duty to fellow men and where they have considerable education, then they can operate political processes which make for change which is peaceful and selective. In the Western democracies, the political institutions have to a great extent been influenced by Christianity. (By Christianity we do not mean clericalism which may be an impediment to peaceful and selective change.) In these countries, conditions approximating those of a free society have on the whole existed for one hundred and fifty years or more. During that period, social and economic change has been so immense that conditions in any one of these countries today would completely bewilder those who lived there one hundred or fifty years ago.

The changes have, in the main, been peaceful changes. There has been little coercion, terrorism, or civil war. The conspicuous apparent exception is the United States war of eighty-five years ago, called in the North the War of the

Rebellion, but in the South the War Between the States. It was, in essence, more international than civil war. The basic issue was whether certain sovereign states had, by prior compact of union, given up the right to resume full sovereignty.

The social changes effected by free political processes have in the main tended to increase the opportunity of the individual to develop according to the dictates of his conscience and reason. Slavery has been abolished. There has been a definite trend away from treating laborers as animals or machines are treated. Women have been freed from grave disabilities. Economically, individual initiative, experimental and competitive, has produced great richness. The Industrial Revolution, while it has brought evils, has shown men how, with less physical effort, they can produce much more. Infant mortality has been greatly reduced, health generally improved, and the span of life lengthened. Education is general, and the development of spiritual life has been kept free of political inhibitions. Graduated income taxes and death duties effect a considerable distribution of production in accordance with need.

To say these things is not to be self-righteous or complacent. There are many great blots and many deficiencies. One notable blot is the persistence in the United States of a considerable, though diminishing, measure of race discrimination. There persist inequities of many kinds, economic, social, and political. There is no assurance that ways have been found to prevent the cyclical breakdown of production process and the vast misery consequent thereon. By no means is God's will done as it is in heaven. To be satisfied would be unchristian.

But it is not unchristian to point out that where political institutions show evidence of Christian influence, the result is good fruit. If that were not so, one could doubt that Christianity did in fact reflect God's ultimate revelation to man. Christ said, "By their fruits ye shall know them." (Matt. 7:20.)

It seems, both on the basis of theoretical reasoning and on the basis of practical experience, that peaceful and selective change can be assured under the conditions of a free society of self-discipline. There is no comparable evidence to show that under a despotic or totalitarian form of society there can be sustained change that is peaceful and selective and which progressively increases the opportunities for individual growth.

WORLD SHORTAGE OF FREE SOCIETIES WITH TESTED POLITICAL INSTITUTIONS

There are not in the world many societies which have tested political mechanisms whereby decisions reflect the choice and reflection of the people as a whole. That, in the main, is not because such institutions are not wanted but because various conditions have militated against their realization. Many peoples have been long in colonial dependency. Some, like the peoples of India and Pakistan and certain Arab states, are only now moving from dependency to full independence. Some, like the peoples of China and Indonesia, are in chaos and strife. Some, like the Germans, Japanese, and Italians, are still under, or just emerging from, the military control of the victors. Some live under constitutions which in words vest sovereignty in the people, but they are, in fact, ruled by a small group which perpetuates itself in power by force, subject to change by periodic revolution. Some live under "dictatorships of the proletariat."

These facts are significant because they affect the practicability of developing internationally processes of change which will be peaceful and selective. It means that there do not exist, on a world-wide scale, tested institutions of political liberty and that there is an absence of the foundation needed for building a world structure which has political power to legislate change. The creation of a world state involves a mechanism of power and the selection of individuals to direct it. If the power is to be sufficient to make possible change which is adequate to replace violent change, there must, somewhere, be large discretionary authority. But it would not be possible today to assure that the discretion would come from peoples who were free, and morally and intellectually trained for the use of political freedom.

Theoretically, it is possible to devise a world representative system so weighted in favor of the societies of tested freedom that their representatives would have the preponderant voice. The others, who are the majority, would never consent to those few societies being accorded world supremacy. They would, in a sense, be justified. For while the free societies have shown good capacity to govern themselves, they have not shown the same good capacity to govern others of different races and cultures. It would not advance us to recreate and extend the colonial system under the guise of world government.

Today any world-wide system for institutionalizing change would inevitably be despotic. Either it would vest arbitrary power in the persons of a few individual officials, or it would vest great power in the small fraction of the human race who have tested political processes for reflecting the individual choice.

The great majority of the world's population will not, and should not, agree to be ruled by the free societies. The free societies will not, and should not, go back under despotism.

This impasse is a source of great peril. It leaves international change to be effected largely by force and coercion. It does so at a time when the means for corrupting men's souls and destroying their bodies have grown far beyond anything that the world has ever known. Thus, Christian citizens can feel that each, according to his means, has a duty to act to increase the possibility of world political unity and processes for peaceful change. That does not mean that Christian citizens will treat unity as the all-sufficient end, to which they should sacrifice what to them seem justice, righteousness, and human dignity. They will seek the conditions for unity with the urgency of those who know that great disaster impends and with the practicability of those who know that such disasters cannot be averted merely by the incantation of fine words.

THE DEVELOPMENT
OF FREE SOCIETIES

If peaceful change requires deciding whose judgment is to prevail, and if the judgment of a free, disciplined society is the only reliable and generally acceptable judgment, then the extension of free societies throughout the world is prerequisite to a world-wide institutionalizing of change. Many Christian citizens see that as the great long-range political task. Its accomplishment would make it possible to set up and operate in a nondespotic way international mechanisms for peaceful change. That task has two aspects:

a. It is first necessary to preserve and improve free societies where they now exist. Free societies are delicate plants. To grow them is a long, hard task and, once they are grown, they are in constant danger of withering away. The postwar climate has been particularly hard on free societies. The cumulative result of two world wars is grave economic distress coupled with great human weariness and disillusionment. Under these conditions, men have a longing to be taken care of. Also, the economic margin for survival has been reduced to a point where centralized planning has seemed necessary. To men who are preoccupied with the struggle for the basic, material needs of life for their families, bread may be of more compelling and immediate importance than civil rights and freedom. Such conditions lead to giving great power to a few men.

Delegation of power does not, of itself, necessarily mean an abandonment of freedom. It may be an exercise of freedom to meet an emergency, and the people may retain both the legal right and the practical political mechanisms for ending the delegation when the emergency has passed. As we have noted, free societies usually give dictatorial powers in time of great emergency, such as war, and it has been shown that they can withstand temporary dictatorship of this kind. Nevertheless, there is always grave risk in conferring dictatorial power because such power can readily become self-perpetuating.

To preserve the characteristics of a free society within the areas where it now measurably prevails will itself be a difficult task. It will require vigilance and dedication by Christians as citizens. That dedication should not be merely in the interest of *preservation,* but of *improvement.* Only effort motivated by the creative urge can generate the needed energy and enthusiasm. Struggles are seldom won merely by a defensive strategy.

b. New free societies must be developed, and this can be done and should be done rapidly wherever the necessary human foundation exists. Fortunately, much has been done through varied channels to create those foundations. The Christian churches have played, in this, a great part. The Christian missionary movement has had a great world-wide influence in developing in men a sense of duty to fellow man. Also, Christian schools and colleges have stimulated education throughout the world. On the moral and educational foundations developed over past generations, much is now being done to erect free political institutions.

Until recently, nearly one third of the world's population were the subject peoples of the free societies. Within the last three years free institutions have been set up in India, Pakistan, Burma, Ceylon, the Philippine Islands, and certain of the Arab states. A large measure of autonomy is envisaged for Indonesia. The total number of peoples thus acquiring political freedom represents about one quarter of the population of the world and could more than double the total population of the free societies. That is an amazing and encouraging occurrence which should confound the pessimists and inspirit the disillusioned.

Of course, it is not certain that all of these new political entities will, in fact, maintain societies of freedom in the full sense. In part the present development represents a great experiment. In many of the areas momentous and difficult decisions remain to be made, and there is not yet the kind and degree of individual moral and intellectual development which would easily assure a peaceful outcome. There will be need of sympathetic understanding, material aid, and scientific and technical assistance from the older societies of freedom.

There remain dependent colonial areas which can be developed toward self-government and free institutions. The colonial powers, by the United Nations Charter, have pledged themselves to seek that development, and to aid in attaining the result, there has been created the Trusteeship Council.

It should be remembered in this connection that political wisdom generally comes only with practical experience. If people are to be held in guardianship until they have fully developed all the qualities desired, there will be an indefinite prolongation of guardianship. It is better to err on the side of giving freedom prematurely than to withhold it until there is demonstrated proof of ability to use it wisely. To learn by self-experience is apt to involve much suffering. But few learn adequately from the experience of others.

There is in China nearly one fifth of the human race. Some Chinese leaders have, in recent years, sought to replace despotism with free political institutions. But progress has been slow. The people are materially impoverished, and only a few have book-learning. They have had to undergo a war and occupation longer than that of the European Continental Allies. Individualism, in terms of the family, is perhaps excessive, and a sense of community too restricted. But the people still possess richly the qualities which will enable them to make a great addition to the foundations of political liberty.

During the last century there developed a sense of fellowship between the Chinese people and the peoples of the West, largely because of the activities of Christian missionaries, educators, and doctors. Now, more than ever, such activities need to be continued and, indeed, intensified.

There is a great responsibility toward the vanquished peoples of Germany, Japan, and Italy. The victors have made themselves the Government of Germany; they, in fact, direct the Government of Japan and will largely influence the postwar development of Italy. The peoples of these countries have education and personal morality in large measure. It ought to be possible for them to develop into free societies. That is a task of great difficulty because of the evil war has bred. But it is a task of unique importance.

A survey of the globe shows that it is possible for upwards of three quarters of the human race to develop peacefully and quickly — say, within one or two generations — the use of free political institutions. No doubt there would be many inadequacies, as indeed there always are. But it is possible to foresee conditions under which there would be obtainable, from most of the peoples of the earth, judgments which reflect the thinking, on an individual basis, of minds and spirits which are free and developed by political experience and self-discipline. On that foundation it would be possible to establish, internationally, procedures for peaceful change which would not be despotic but which would reflect that moral sense which, we believe, is potential in every human being.

The program suggested has a particular appeal to Christians because it is a peaceful program to which the Christian churches can make a great contribution. There can be parallel effort by the churches and Christian citizens.

The free society cannot be equated with a Christian society, and it is possible to have free societies whose institutions are predominantly influenced by non-Christian religions. But the Christian faith especially emphasizes those qualities of self-control and love of neighbor which are needed for the good operation of a free society. So, Christian citizens could feel that to extend free societies was a great long-range effort to which they could worthily dedicate themselves and seek to dedicate their nations. Thereby they would be laying the indispensable foundation for world institutions for peaceful and selective change. Those engaged in that effort could feel that they were making the world more nearly one where God's

will would be done, and they would be responsive to the appeal
of the masses that a way be found to save them and their
children from the death, the misery, the starvation of body
and soul which recurrent violence now wreaks upon man.

◇◇◇◇

[*Here followed a discussion in some detail of the then pre-
vailing problems posed by the policies of the Soviet Union.*]

◇◇◇◇

PEACEFUL RECONCILIATION OF PROGRAM
WITH SOVIET PROGRAM

The Soviet reliance on change by force and violence con-
stitutes a serious obstacle athwart our suggested program.
Soviet influence is considerable, and it is now favored by external conditions. World War II created a vacuum of power
in many areas. Of the eight so-called great powers, three —
Italy, Germany, and Japan — have been engulfed by the disaster of defeat. Three —United Kingdom, France, and China
— have been enfeebled by the struggle for victory. Therefore,
there is about the Soviet Union a power vacuum into which
it has already moved to bring some three hundred million
people, representing about fifteen nationalities, under the
dominant influence of dictatorship of the proletariat and its
revolutionary theories and practices.

Even more important than this fact of political vacuum is
the fact that there has developed in the world much of a
moral vacuum. The so-called Western or Christian civilization
has long accepted most of the social ends now professed by
the Soviet Communist Party and, indeed, its goals have been
even more advanced. But of recent years it has seemed to be
halfhearted and lacking in fervor or sense of urgency. The result has been that many people have unthinkingly compared
the idealized purposes and theories of the Soviet program

with the worst practices of Western nations. Others, eager for quick results, uncritical of means, have been attracted to the Soviet program by the very violence of its means, which have seemed a proof of zeal. The fact that Christian citizens tend to favor nonviolent means is taken as proof that they lack zeal. The consequent degree of following attracted by the Soviet dynamic program has encouraged Soviet leaders to entertain great expectations of realizing their particular "one world." Their ambitions have mounted so that there is indeed grave danger of that "series of frightful collisions between the Soviet Republic and the bourgeois states" which Lenin and Stalin have forecast as inevitable.

Christians must dedicate themselves to prevent such developments. There are in the main two ways of doing so.

First, Christians must reject, and see to it that their nations reject, the Soviet thesis of the inevitability of violent conflict, and they must not imitate Soviet leadership by placing reliance on violent means.

Secondly, Christians must see to it that their nations demonstrate that peaceful methods can realize the goals which we all espouse.

There is disturbing evidence that the so-called free societies are themselves tending to adopt those features of Soviet procedure which Christians particularly condemn. In the United States great emphasis is being placed upon achieving military supremacy, and military counsels are more influential than has normally been the case in that republic. Some portions of the American press are stirring up emotional hatred against the Soviet Union, and there is some distortion of truth, principally through the exaggeration of what is true but of minor importance. . . .

◇◇◇◇

The most important response to the Soviet challenge will be in effecting peacefully the reforms which Soviet leaders contend can only be effected by violent means. We must by actual demonstration disprove Stalin's dictum that "one must be a revolutionary, not a reformist."

The Western democracies won their prestige in the world through their great peaceful accomplishments. The Industrial Revolution, the concept of "liberty, equality, and fraternity," and the experiments in political freedom created world-wide confidence in the dynamic and life-giving quality of their institutions. But for long now these democracies have faced no serious competition. The quality of their effort has deteriorated, and they have, to a considerable extent, been coasting with a momentum that is waning. Many do not like it that a challenge has now arisen. Many would prefer peace which is a condition of tranquillity or stagnation, where all threat and challenge are removed and where men can feel that they can safely relax. Some are inclined to the view that unless we get that kind of peace, we do not have peace at all, and an irresponsible few talk of using force to crush the challenger. That is folly. Those of us who are of the Western peoples face the task of mental adjustment to a dynamic peace where there is competition. We need to make it clear to ourselves and we need to make it clear to proponents of other systems that we welcome a world in which there is peaceful competition. Above all, we need to make it clear that we can peacefully, through reform, bring about results which all men want, and which they will be apt to seek by the violent methods which the Soviet sponsors, unless we can prove that they can be achieved by peaceful means.

Whenever a system is challenged, there is a tendency to rally to support the system as is. The world becomes divided between those who would maintain the *status quo* and those who would change the *status quo*. As we have seen, those who would sustain the *status quo* inevitably are defeated. And almost inevitably the issue is resolved by violence. The result may not be the particular changes desired by the dynamic powers, but equally, it does not maintain the status which their opponents sought to preserve. So it is that in the face of Soviet challenge we must not rally to the defense of our institutions just as they are, but we must seek even more ardently to make them better than what they now are.

In fact, much progress has been made along this line. We have already referred to the action of Great Britain in bringing about five hundred millions of colonial dependent peoples peacefully to self-government. That has been the most effective way to demonstrate that the achievement of self-government by dependent peoples was not dependent upon a Soviet "revolutionary alliance," and that it is possible to achieve by peaceful means results which the Soviet leaders profess to want but which they have said could only be achieved by violent means.

The free societies have also made considerable progress in achieving an economy whereby production is on the basis of ability and distribution on the basis of need. The steeply graduated income and estate taxes which now prevail generally in capitalistic countries take largely from those who have ability to accumulate, and to an increasing extent this is being distributed to those in need in the form of Social Security programs. These countries are in fact much closer to the so-called higher phase of communism than is the Soviet Union itself.

Socially, the great blot on the escutcheon of the democracies is the discrimination against colored persons practiced by much of the white population of the United States. Here, however, the problem is recognized, and great efforts are being made to deal with it. It is not possible by legislative fiat to eradicate social prejudices, the origins of which go back hundreds of years. There is, however, a vast change which is in peaceful process.

The danger is that those who face the Soviet challenge will feel they must defend themselves on every count. There is some evidence that the Soviet challenge is, to an extent, having that natural result. Christians must stand strong against that, recognizing the imperfection of every system and of every nation, not identifying righteousness with anything that is, but constantly striving to prove that the evils that exist can be eradicated by peaceful means. . . .

◇◇◇◇

The years between the Soviet Revolution and World War II involved a very large exposure of practical bankruptcy on the part of non-Communist nations. During that period the free societies, at least, were not at their best. Soviet leaders have encountered weaknesses which have afforded them great opportunities and given them great encouragement. Within recent years that situation has begun to change. There have been some great constructive developments. To some of these we have alluded. It is possible to push forward along these lines and it is imperative that this should be done. . . .

◇◇◇◇

The Soviet challenge loses its potency once the free societies show a capacity for constructive action. As we have said, the challenge in its present phase seems not a militaristic challenge, like that of Hitler, Mussolini, and the Japanese war lords. It is a call to revolution. If the non-Communist societies, faced by that challenge, stand still and do nothing, for fear of offending Soviet leadership, they are lost. If they quietly move ahead, showing a practical capacity to achieve peacefully the things which Soviet leaders say can come only after an "entire historical era" of violence, then those talkers will quickly be rated as "incorrigible windbags" — to use Stalin's expression.

It is important that there be these peaceful developments both domestically and internationally. We have already outlined what might be the grand, over-all, international program. But such a long-range program is not enough to meet the present need because it does not contain enough possibility to register quickly decisive results and thus to create general recognition of the capacity of the free societies. Intermediate programs are needed, where successes can be registered, prestige gained, and momentum acquired. We shall go on to consider what might be some of these intermediate programs.

INTERMEDIATE STEPS PRESENTLY PRACTICABLE

It is not necessary to stand still and do nothing internationally until there has been laid the world-wide foundation for a free world society. There is much which can be done, today and tomorrow. There are already two great assets with which to work. One is the great and all-pervading force of the moral law. A second is the existence of an organization — the United Nations — which brings together in public association most of the nations of the world. On the basis of these two facts, many intermediate successes can be achieved.

The moral law has universal influence. There are some who deny its existence and who try to educate men to ignore it. It is never immediately and universally effective. But still there is general, world-wide agreement about right and wrong in their broad outlines. That fact is of immense importance, for it makes it possible to use moral force for peace and justice at a time when there cannot yet be an adequate political mechanism.

Moral power can be a powerful force in the world. That is not a mere pious hope. It is the judgment of every realist throughout history. It was Napoleon who said that "in war, moral considerations make up three fourths of the game." It was Admiral Mahan who said that physical force was useful only "to give moral ideals time to take root."

Allied leaders during both the First and Second World Wars did much to consolidate and marshal world sentiment to insure Germany's defeat. They did that through great statements of aims, such as the Fourteen Points and the Atlantic Charter, which appealed to the moral conscience of the world. It is possible also to frame issues and organize moral power in the interest of peace.

The United Nations is a political machine which even now can be used to make moral power work during peace to preserve peace. That is largely due to Christian influence.

Many thought that world organization should be primarily a military organization to carry out the will of the great powers. That was, indeed, the conception which dominated the representatives of the Soviet Union, Great Britain, and the United States when they met at Dumbarton Oaks in the summer of 1944 to make a first draft of the Charter. But our church people did not think much of an organization which would be primarily military and which would depend chiefly on physical force. So they worked hard to make their point of view prevail. It did largely prevail at the San Francisco Conference of 1945, thanks in great part to the small nations, which did not want to be placed permanently under the military dictatorship of the three big powers.

So the San Francisco Conference radically changed the plan of Dumbarton Oaks. It emphasized the United Nations General Assembly as a place where the representatives of all states, big and little, would meet and discuss any problems of international relations, and where even the great nations could be required to subject their conduct to the judgment of world opinion.

The United Nations has now been functioning for over two years. Many are disappointed with the results. They would like the United Nations to be able to dictate and enforce the particular results which they want. As we have seen, the United Nations cannot now be that kind of an organization. However, it has revealed great possibilities. Of course it has not settled everything. Indeed, the international situation is gravely troubled. But the United Nations has shown that it need not be a mere spectator. It can do something. It can call every nation's international acts to the bar of public opinion, with confidence that that will have healthy practical consequences.

We have seen how, in time of war, the public verdict of right and wrong exercises a powerful effect. The United Nations has begun to show how, in time of peace, public opinion can exercise a powerful effect. At the San Francisco Conference and at the subsequent Assemblies of the United Nations, political leaders from many lands have presented views on many matters. Always the speakers were obviously conscious of the fact that their audience included the representatives of many million people who possessed great power and who were primarily swayed by moral considerations. Every speaker presented his case with regard to what he thought was world opinion, and he tried to get its backing. Almost always the different Governments presented their positions otherwise than they would have done had they been meeting in secret and not subject to informed world opinion. That is a fact of great moment. It does not make future war impossible. It can make war less likely. . . .

◇◇◇◇

So, while the United Nations cannot today be converted into a mechanism directed by a few persons having power to rule the nations, it can be used to subject national acts to the test of moral judgment. Moral power arises from the most humble to reach the most mighty. It works inexorably, even though slowly. It will not suit the impatient. But it can achieve solid results. The important thing is that the United Nations be used for purposes for which it is adapted and not be discredited by attempted use for purposes for which it is ill adapted. . . .

◇◇◇◇

[Here followed a series of specific suggestions for the more effective functioning of the United Nations.]

◇◇◇◇

We could go on indefinitely in this vein. We have, however, said enough to indicate that, with a moral law of universal scope and with the United Nations as a place to bring together national acts and world-wide judgments, important intermediate results can be achieved. There is much to be done on a less than universal basis, within the framework of the Charter. Nations and peoples can do much to help each other. Such efforts do not take the place of our long-range program because they do not constitute a conscious, planned effort to create, on a world-wide basis, the conditions prerequisite to a general institutionalizing of change. But interim measures can gain the time and the prestige needed for successful development of a long-range program.

What seems urgent — and possible — is to revive in men a sense of moving peacefully toward a state of greater perfection. Many have been beaten and broken in spirit by the violence of the forces that have been loose in the world for now upward of a decade. They temporarily placed hope — perhaps undue hope — in the United Nations. But that hope has largely gone, and there is despairing acceptance of the idea that continuing violence is inevitable for an entire historical era.

That is a dangerous mood. It can, perhaps, be broken by acts which, even in a small way, show the possibility of peaceful change. Let us, therefore, not despise what is presently possible, knowing that out of small things can come a rebirth of faith and hope, and that out of faith and hope can come great things, far beyond any that are here portrayed.

CONCLUSION
The Role of the Christian Church

Many will feel that the programs here outlined are quite inadequate; and those who feel that way may be quite right. . . . We have tried to write under a self-imposed ordinance, namely, to propose only what we felt might *practically* be achieved by *peaceful* means and without the sacrifice of hard-won human rights. No doubt, even within this limitation, there are better prospects than are here portrayed. But no program which is both practical and peaceful will seem as exciting and dramatic as a program which is purely imaginative or violent. . . .

◇◇◇◇

We are fully conscious of the fact that peaceful and practical programs will seem to many to evidence a lack of zeal and to conceal a desire selfishly to preserve the evils of the *status quo*. That appraisal, in our opinion, can be and should be changed. Christians should, we believe, appraise more highly than they seem to do the self-control, the self-discipline, and the respect for human dignity required to make change peaceful. The Christian churches could, we think, find the way to make peaceful efforts seem more inspirational and be more sacrificial. It is a tragedy that inspiration and sacrifice in large volume seem to be evoked only by ways of violence. If the Christian churches could change that, then, indeed, they would help the Christian citizen along his way.

We have not outlined tasks which could be participated in only by Christians because we believe that if Christians advance a political program which only Christians can support, they logically must contemplate a monopoly of power and privilege on behalf of their particular sect. That, we have made clear, would in our opinion vitiate the program. But the task which we have outlined is a task which should arouse the Christian churches to a sense of special responsibility.

What is the need? The need is for men and women who can see what now is and what can be. Christ put particular emphasis on vision and light. He taught men to see truly and to avoid the hatred, hypocrisy, and selfishness which blind men or warp their visions. If Christian churches do not produce the needed vision, what can we expect but that mankind will stumble?

The need is for men who have the peacefulness which comes to those who are possessed by the Christian spirit of love, who have the power which comes to those who pray, repent, and are transformed, and who have the dedication of those who leave all to follow Him.

The need is for more effective political use of moral power. The moral law, happily, is a universal law. But Christians believe that, through Christ, the moral law has been revealed with unique clarity. The Christian churches ought, therefore, to be especially qualified to help men to form moral judgments which are discerning and to focus them at the time and place where they can be effective.

The need is for full use of the present great possibilities of the United Nations. It was Christians most of all who wanted a world organization which would depend primarily on moral, rather than physical, power. They have it. Now it is up to the churches to generate the moral power required to make the organization work.

The need is to build the foundation for a more adequate world organization. A world of free societies could be that foundation, and free society depends in turn on individuals who exemplify Christian qualities of self-control and of human brotherhood, and who treat freedom, not as license, but as occasion for voluntary co-operation for the common good. So, again, the Christian churches have the great responsibility.

The need is for effort on a world-wide scale. The Christian church is a world-wide institution. Consequently, the individual Christian may exert his influence not only as a citizen but also as member of a church which in its corporate life has a contribution to make. The church demonstrates in its own life the achievement of community out of various races, nationalities, and communions. It develops a common ethos. Its missionary movement constantly extends the fellowship of those who share the same loyalties and purposes. Its ecumenical movement deepens and consolidates that fellowship.

Its program of relief and reconstruction restores hope to the despairing and reconciles those who have been enemies. The Commission of the Churches on International Affairs is beginning to give stimulus and leadership to the more direct impact of the churches on the current problems of relations between the nations. Thus the churches themselves in many ways can help build the bases for world order.

So it is that, as we analyze the need, Christian responsibility emerges as an inescapable fact. It is a fact that ought to have practical consequences. The potentialities of Christian influence are great, but the present weight of Christian impact is wholly inadequate. If, in the international field, Christians are to play their clearly indicated part, their churches must have better organization, more unity of action, and put more emphasis on Christianity as a world religion. That, we pray, will come from the Amsterdam Assembly and the final realization of the World Council of Churches.

19

Leadership for Peace

WE MEET at a time that is reminiscent of 1939. In January of that year the President, in a message to Congress, warned that "freedom of religion has been attacked" and that "the attack has come from sources opposed to democracy." He called for increased Armed Forces because the "probability of attack is mightily decreased by the assurance of an ever-ready defense," and he said that we must make effective protest against aggressors although, he said, "obviously along practical, peaceful lines." Two years later we were in the thick of World War II.

Many today feel that history is repeating itself and that forces beyond our control are irresistibly dragging us into another war.

War is not inevitable, but thinking that it is can make it so. Concededly, there are in the world today, as in 1939, forces that oppose religious freedom and democracy and that are aggressively disposed. But there always have been, and always will be, such forces in the world. International peace, like

---

Address opening the National Study Conference on the Churches and World Order, Cleveland, Ohio, March 8, 1949.

domestic peace, does not have to await the total eradication of evil.

Already in 1940 our churches foresaw that the destruction of the Nazi regime would not end for all time such evils as were in nazism and automatically bring lasting peace. They knew that such evils were recurrent. So they set up a special organization to help them bring new elements into being so that, after World War II, it might be possible to counter peacefully the forces of disorder. The churches wanted the postwar situation to be different for the very reason that they did not want history to repeat itself.

We have to a large extent succeeded. Today there are assets for peace which were wholly lacking before World War II. The present perils are great, but if it were possible to trade what now is for what then was, none, I hope, would make that barter.

After the First World War it seemed that the nations made peace very quickly. Only seven months after the Armistice, the Treaty of Versailles had been completed, in order, as it is there said, to replace the state of war "by a firm, just, and durable peace." The League of Nations was established. The Washington Conference on Naval Limitation reflected the will of the victors to reduce their armament, and the Kellogg-Briand Pact outlawed war. On the surface, all seemed well. But beneath the sugar-coating of fine words there was much that was unsavory.

The American people, who even then possessed preponderant power in the world, turned soft, sentimental, and undisciplined. We abandoned what Washington called "a respectable defensive posture" not as a matter of principle or considered policy but because we found that posture uncomfortable. We adopted an attitude of illusory aloofness. We refused to join the League of Nations, and we sought to enclose our economy and be an oasis of prosperity in a world of misery. We were without vision and did not see that the revolutionary theories of Marx had found powerful embodiment in Russia and that misery and despair in Germany were breeding nazism. We were fascinated by the beautiful things that could be done with words and thought that great results could be accomplished quickly without hard work.

So in 1939 when our nation belatedly bestirred itself for peace, its leadership was without the moral, economic, and military assets that were needed to make its influence felt. At least that is what our leaders told us.

Today matters are different. The United States has not relapsed into a state of supineness. We are maintaining a powerful military establishment, even though that involves substantial sacrifice. . . .

Our nation has achieved a new level of peacetime productivity and also the willingness to share with others. . . .

The United States took leadership in creating a world organization and is taking a leading part in that organization. Our Government is willing to make the United Nations stronger as quickly as that can be done without destroying its universal character. In the meantime, our country has joined an American hemisphere regional pact that involves some surrender of sovereignty, and a comparable Atlantic Pact is in the making.

Our eyes are open to what is going on in the world. Perhaps sometimes we so strain our vision that it distorts what it sees, but at least we are neither blind nor purely introspective.

We are largely cured of the illusion that words are a substitute for deeds, and we know that a just and durable peace cannot be achieved merely by writing it or by heads of state meeting to proclaim it.

All in all, the American people have gone far to correct what they were told were the deficiencies that made it impossible to prevent World War II. Then, it seemed, the people gave would-be peacemakers only bricks without straw. Now they have given some solid brick. Political leadership thus has possibilities that formerly were denied it — and a correspondingly greater accountability.

Our churches have played a notable part in changing the attitudes of our people.

In 1942, at our First National Study Conference at Delaware, there was drawn up the Statement of Guiding Principles. That emphasized the heavy responsibility that devolved upon the United States. "If the future," we said, "is to be other than a repetition of the past, the United States must accept the responsibility for constructive action commensurate with its power and opportunity."

We next drew up, in application of the Guiding Principles, a Statement of Political Propositions generally known as the Six Pillars of Peace. There we set forth the necessity of creating a world organization and outlined the essential tasks that should be given it. That was at a time when our political leadership had not yet felt that world organization was feasible and when reference to it had deliberately been excluded from the statement of peace aims embodied in the Atlantic Charter.

In 1945, when the Dumbarton Oaks Proposals for world organization had been drafted, our Second National Study

Conference exposed certain basic omissions in those proposals, notably in relation to justice, law, human rights, and self-government for colonial peoples, and we sought and largely obtained a moral reorientation of the Charter. Also, we then committed ourselves to renounce the escapist idealism that had been widely prevalent after World War I. We pointed out that "an idealism which does not accept the discipline of the achievable may lose its power for good."

In 1946, we issued a Statement on Soviet-American Relations. We pointed out the impossibility of compromise on matters of faith, but asserted that "war with Russia can be avoided and it must be avoided without compromise of basic convictions." We went on to show that irreconcilable beliefs could coexist in a peaceful world so long as believers renounced the use of violence, coercion, or terrorism to make their faith prevail. That diagnosis, with its key to peace, has now been widely accepted, as shown by the debates at the last Assembly of the United Nations.

In 1947, before there was a European Recovery Program, we said that "Christian precept and enlightened self-interest call for United States economic aid to a degree not yet understood or accepted by our people." And after the European Recovery Program had been formulated, we rallied our church people to support that program in "the conviction that it can be one of history's most momentous affirmations of faith in the curative power of freedom and in the creative capacity of free men."

In April of last year, at a period of great nervousness, when it seemed to many that war with Russia was imminent and unavoidable, we issued a steadying statement calling upon our people to reject fatalism about war and to contribute, each of them, to a change of mood.

I refer to this series of statements not because I, too, have fallen a victim to the illusion that results are achieved merely by fine words, but because every one of these statements, issued at a decisive moment, was carried into the thinking and acting of millions of our citizens by means of publications, study conferences, national missions on world order, and other denominational and interdenominational efforts. At times we worked side by side with Roman Catholics and with Jews. We did not attempt to intermingle church and state; nor did we seek to have the churches make authoritative pronouncements with respect to detailed action in the political field. But we have tried to make clear what Christian principles meant in terms of the actual problems Christians faced as citizens. We have done that sufficiently, so that what we did has had practical consequences.

If our nation has abandoned political isolation, it is largely because our Christian people took the lead in developing the public opinion that not only permitted but that compelled our Government to work to establish a world organization and to work with it. If our nation has abandoned economic isolation, it is because our Christian people saw that both morality and enlightened self-interest required that we who were strong ought to help those who were weak. If our nation is armed, it is because our Christian people, for the most part, have not sought unilateral disarmament. And if, over the past three years, our nation has dealt with the Soviet Union on a basis that has been firm but that, for the most part, avoided provocation, it is largely because our Christian people have, on the one hand, seen the danger lying behind beguiling communist propaganda, but have also seen that there was no inevitability of war.

◈◈

The fact that Christian influence has affected our national conduct is nothing novel, nor should it be surprising. All students of United States history agree that our institutions became what they are, and that our national conduct has been what it was, primarily because of the religious views of our people respecting such matters as the nature of man, the moral law, and the mission of men and nations. Some of the present generation have not learned their history — or have forgotten it. They seem to think it necessary to devise new ways to make America a force for righteousness. What has counted over the past, and what counts today, is the powerhouse of faith and the transmission lines that connect faith and practices.

I know of my personal knowledge the profound influence that has been exerted upon Government by the public opinion that the churches have created over recent years. Most of our political leaders are themselves God-fearing men, who welcome religious influence. Of course there are a few who fear it. They think that it leads to sentimentality and impracticality. They think that they would like it better if the churches confined themselves to ritualistic worship and left it wholly to Government, through its propaganda, to create the public opinion that it thinks is needed to assure the ends that it thinks best.

No doubt the Christian influence is sometimes unrealistic and it does not always accept the discipline of the achievable. No doubt it sometimes annoys those who have the responsibility for practical action and sometimes it intrudes without good reason. Some will probably be annoyed with what we do here, and others will find it inconvenient to reckon with an opinion inspired by what we believe to be sources higher than Government. But that is petty stuff compared to the great fact that the American people do have a faith. No people are ever great, even in worldly terms, without a faith, and nothing would be more dangerous and destructive than to have the present great material power of the United States rattling around in the world detached from the guiding direction of a righteous faith.

The problem on which we plan to center our thinking at this Conference is how our nation can discharge its tremendous responsibility in the world today. We have, in the past, glimpsed that responsibility, but today we see that its magnitude far exceeds our earlier imaginings. The end of the war left us with economic productivity almost equal to that of all of the rest of the world combined. We are the only non-Communist state capable of balancing the military power of the Soviet Union, which otherwise would be dominant in the world. We have moral authority because it is generally believed that we have no lust for conquest, that we genuinely desire peace, and that we may have the wisdom and self-control needed to bring to the world an assurance of peace. All of the non-Communist nations look to us for leadership, and without that leadership there will be chaos in the world.

There can be little doubt but what our nation must accept the leadership that events press into our hands, and at this National Study Conference we shall consider what that means in terms of our relations toward the Soviet Union, toward Europe, toward the Far East and toward the United Nations. I shall not at this time begin that discussion, but I shall suggest certain basic qualities that, it seems to me, our leadership should possess.

1. *First of all, our leadership should be a leadership of peace, by peace, for peace.* That is not a demand for peace at

any price. There are some things that, to many, are more precious than peace. Our Constitutional Bill of Rights assumes that willingness and ability to use arms "are necessary to the security of a free state." But that is something very different from leadership that is on friendly terms with war.

There are some who talk about war as though it were an unpleasant but necessary remedy for existing ills. The fact is that another world war would plunge all of humanity into a pit too awful to contemplate, and make it almost impossible to achieve the good ends for which, no doubt, the combatants would profess to be fighting. It was World War I that delivered the two hundred million people of Russia to the dictatorship of the Communist Party, and World War II is delivering perhaps seven hundred million more people to that control. In a war climate, human liberty wilts, and totalitarianism spreads like a green bay tree. No one who is sincerely anticommunist can be complacent about war unless passion dominates his reason. . . .

◇◇◇◇

Calm analysis justifies the conclusion that, under present circumstances, war is neither useful nor inevitable and whether or not it comes depends most of all on the quality of United States leadership. With all of the assets, moral and material, of which it now disposes, our leadership ought to be able to assure peace. The old alibis have been swept away and if, today, the world passes into the blackness of another war, our leadership cannot escape a large measure of responsibility. That sobering thought should lift our nation above the sway of passion that makes fools the equals of the wise.

2. *Our leadership must be prepared to take some chances for peace.* Winning peace is not just a matter of good intentions. It involves difficult decisions and hard choices. At times,

it may even be necessary to risk war to win peace. Therefore, military considerations are never negligible. At times, military advantage can be gained at the cost of diminishing somewhat the prospect of peace. Sometimes a given course of action may increase somewhat the prospect of peace, but at the cost of putting our nation in a somewhat less advantageous position to win a war should it come. Peace may depend on who makes such decisions — civilians trained in the art of peace or soldiers trained in the art of war.

There are no finer, more patriotic, more personally peace-loving citizens than most of those in our Armed Services. However, they have a distinctive professional responsibility, and that is to do whatever lies within their power to make sure that if there is war, they will win it. That is their job and that is their training. They do not know how to use, perhaps powerfully, perhaps delicately, the enormous possibilities for peace that reside in moral and economic forces, in organizations like the United Nations and the World Court, and in the resources of diplomacy and conciliation. They do not know how to appraise those possibilities. That, too, is an art, and only those skilled in it are qualified to calculate the risks that must be taken for peace, just as only soldiers are competent, in war, to calculate the risks that have to be taken for victory. If we try to give the military the responsibility of preserving peace, they are apt to muff it because it is not the kind of responsibility for which they are trained.

Furthermore, history shows that whenever a nation has a great military establishment, it is under a powerful temptation to rely on the use, or the pressure, of that power, to gain its ends. The greater a nation's military establishment is, the greater should be the gulf between its military leaders and the making of national policy.

Under present conditions, it may be that a strong U.S. military establishment can serve the interest of peace. But that assumes what General Eisenhower refers to as "the necessary and wise subordination of the military to civil power." That is traditional American principle, and failure to observe it will, I fear, not serve the cause of peace.

I can assure you that the peoples and Governments of other lands who proffer us world leadership, do not do so because they want to help us *win* a war with Russia. They do it in order that there should *not be* a war. We would be false to ourselves and false to the trust that mankind puts in our leadership if we allow military judgments to be dominant in our national policy.

3. *Our peaceful leadership must be positive and not merely negative.* . . . It is not possible, in these matters, to be dogmatic or wholly to ignore strategic considerations, but, generally speaking, we should be selective in our moral and material support. We need not laud or sanctify whatever or whomever communism attacks, and our material support should principally serve to sustain, fortify, and enlarge human freedom and healthy economic and social conditions. We should have our own plan of campaign and not let Soviet Communism make it for us.

There was a time when the Western democracies were supreme in prestige because of their dynamic pursuit of liberty, equality, and fraternity, their great experiments in political freedom, and their Industrial Revolution which multiplied many times the productivity of human effort.

It is time to recapture that initiative and we can, in that connection, welcome President Truman's proposal for a pooling of technological resources for the advancement of backward areas.

There is no policy so barren, so certain to fail, as that of maintaining the *status quo.* If our leadership is to be successful, it must develop constructive and creative programs that will capture the imagination and enlist the support of the multitudes whose interest in battling political, economic, and racial injustice is greater than their interest in defending such injustice merely because communism attacks it.

4. *Our leadership must be one of fellowship and not of mastery.* In much of the world, the word "leader" has acquired an ugly significance. Nazism was founded on the "leader" principle. The Communist Party operates under the principle of iron discipline, with a pitiless purging of all who deviate from what the party leaders prescribe. Throughout the world, millions have been bruised in body and spirit by leadership that has meant the ruthless mastery of a brutal few.

Western leadership, too, is under suspicion. For centuries, the West enjoyed a world-wide political supremacy that had elements of economic exploitation and racial intolerance. That supremacy is now peacefully withering away and giving place to self-government. Within recent years over five hundred million people have passed from colonial to self-governing status, and an equal number have been released from Western ties that, in fact, were political shackles. It is to the honor of Western civilization that its Christian ideals and its economic enterprise made possible this peaceful evolution. Nevertheless, the motives of the West have, in the past, been sufficiently selfish, so that today many of other races and cultures are fearful lest the West take advantage of this crisis and use its superior economic and military power to regain world mastery.

They want us to lead, but they want leadership that combines with fellowship. They accept that we have a certain primacy, but only the kind of primacy that can exist as between equals.

That is where the United Nations comes in. It is organized as a center for harmonizing the actions of nations on the basis of the sovereign equality of all its members. We meet there, and discuss, in fellowship. Ideas are valued on the basis of merit, and not merely on the basis of the power of the nation from which they emanate.

There are some matters that, because of their nature, cannot be effectively or properly dealt with through the United Nations. But experience has shown that the United Nations could be trusted much more than has been the case. We can, and should, make the Charter a framework within which our leadership will be exercised in fellowship.

5. *Finally, our leadership should be compassionately human.* Let us not forget that what our nation *is,* is just as important as what it does. There come times which seem to call for action. The present seems one of those times. . . . We devise machines to calculate flights of missiles that are beyond human calculation. We perform miracles of production through the use of ever more efficient tools. Such action may be necessary, and there are many whose duty it is to engage in it. But there is about all this a certain hardness that can affect the inner soul.

What is our feverishness about? It is presumably to save mankind from falling under the sway of a materialistic rule that holds that man's chief end is to glorify the state and to serve it forever. But we shall not accomplish that great and worthy purpose if we go about it in such a way that we, too, become inhuman and deaf to the cry of the masses that a way be found to save them and their children from the death, the misery, the starvation of body and soul that recurrent war and economic disorder now wreak upon man.

Sometimes our churches try to do that for which they are not equipped, neglecting their own distinctive tasks. Today one of the churches' tasks is to preserve in our nation human sympathy and compassion such as Jesus had when he saw the multitudes.

If our churches perform that task, the other problems that concern our nation will more readily be solved. Then our leadership is bound to be leadership that seeks peace; our programs will assuredly be designed to increase human welfare and our relations with others will be those of fellowship. And then perhaps it may be said to our nation: "Thy faith hath saved thee; go in peace."

20

The Way of Love and Compassion

I AM GRATEFUL to you for inviting me to join with the friends
of the Presbyterian Hospital. I am proud of the long identification of my family with this institution of healing, compassion, and loving care.

These are qualities that life compels everyone to need; and
when that need arises, as it implacably does, no material
wealth, no political power, no brilliance of mind is any substitute for these gifts of the soul which others can bestow.

Of course, material things have their worth. Without money
and scientific knowledge we would not have this hospital and
its equipment. But material things get their value primarily
from the spiritual values that go with them and from dedication to uses, inspired by hearts that are responsive to the two
great commandments to love God and to love fellow man.

At first thought, it seems strange that the most valuable
things are not things which need be scarce but rather are
spiritual qualities which each and every one of us can possess
abundantly, and which each can give away and still be the
richer. But, on reflection, is it not plain that that is the wondrous miracle of our world and the final proof that the world

---

Address at the Presbyterian Hospital, Philadelphia, April 14, 1952.

is a spiritual world, not made by man? Would not this world be an unjust world if the most valuable things were so scarce that only a few could possess them? It is typical of a man-made order that the greatest value is put on scarcity. But man cannot change the scale of values that God ordained. He in his infinite wisdom and justice made a world where no accident of birth or circumstance limits the capacity of each person to give and to receive the most precious things of life. No one is so poor, so illiterate, and so low in the social scale that he cannot give; no one is so rich, so brainy, or so powerful that he does not need what even the weakest can give him.

No one has given greatly if he has given only materially, and no one is rich unless he receives from others the spiritual values that they have to give.

Constantly, I am in receipt of letters from those who inquire as to what they can do to make this world a better world. They can, whoever they are, give love, sympathy, and compassionate understanding of their fellow men, near and far. And they can, in turn, attract from others the good will, the sympathetic understanding, which enriches those who receive.

In the intimacy of our family and within our homes we realize and practice these truths. We know that the pains of birth, illness, disappointment, and finally death are made tolerable by loving care, and that the joys of life are intensified by sympathetic sharing. Sometimes we forget that what is true in detail is also true in mass. In the family of nations the needs and the values are the same.

The present extremity of trouble within the nations is not due primarily to a shortage of material things. Of course there are such shortages, but they are relatively less today than ever before in the world's history. The troubles are primarily due to the fact that more than ever before political influence is being exerted by those who think and act in terms that are calculated on a purely material basis.

The great evil of Soviet Communism, which dominates one third of the globe, is that it puts material things first. As Stalin has said in his essay on dialectical and historical materialism, "The material life of society is primary, and its spiritual life secondary." . . .

◇◇◇◇

But we in America, who have leadership in the world that is free, are ourselves not without fault. We are relatively free of the fanatical intolerance which characterizes Soviet Communism. But we are apt to look upon our great material possessions with pride as themselves proving us to be superior people. The fact is that this superiority in material things is not nearly so important as many of us believe, and we learn that to our dismay when we deal with other peoples. We think that they should admire us because we have more automobiles than all of the rest of the world put together. We think they should be grateful to us because in one form or another we have given away nearly fifty billion dollars since the fighting stopped. We think that others are stupid and ungrateful that they do not bow down before such material magnificence.

The fact is that our mechanical gadgets are not in the main what others want. Indeed, these others may possess in greater measure than do we ourselves the values which our Christian religion teaches are supreme.

Among other peoples—the Japanese, the Indians, the Mexicans, to name only a few — there are many who possess a love and appreciation of beauty, a capacity for human understanding, and a richness of sympathy which we might well covet for ourselves. If we apply a true measuring rod, we will approach them humbly and not in a mood of lofty superiority.

Also, while what we have given is important, it has not involved either giving or receiving the spiritual values that count most. We have not given out of compassion or because of love of our fellow men. Our vast public loans and grants to other nations have been made, not because we wanted to make them, but because we have been told that we had to make them in order to achieve certain political objectives. The gifts have not carried a message of sympathy and good will but rather expressions of annoyance, grumbling, and carping criticism. The result is that we have not gotten what we bargained for. Our nation is today less liked, more isolated, and more endangered than ever before in its history.

I recall the moving plea which Charles Malik of Lebanon made at the Japanese Peace Conference on behalf of the Near East: "Believe me, I weigh every word when I say our problems, overwhelming as they are, can be solved, and a wondrous new era can usher in, in the Near East, if only people care enough." Apparently no one has cared enough, for that plea has gone without response for now nearly eight months.

Do we care and shall we act out of caring? That is the vital question that confronts our people. Jesus, when he saw the multitudes, was moved with compassion, and then he gave them some material help. He did not give that help because he had calculated that it would be good political propaganda. That is the way for us to follow, making the spiritual primary and the material secondary. That is indeed the traditional American way, and I believe that the American people are eager to return to that way.

I think they would like to do what they believe is the right thing to do rather than constantly be doing what they are told is an act of political expediency.

If only we care enough and have compassion and act as that spirit directs, then our position in the world would be revolutionized overnight. Then, I predict, we shall get, as a by-product, the security which eludes us so long as we seek it in selfish calculation.

It is everlastingly true that if we seek first the Kingdom of God and his righteousness, these other things will be added unto us.

21

The Significance of Theological Education

OUT IN Tennessee there is a plant which turns out bombs. Here we have a plant which turns out ministers of the gospel. The two seem remote and unrelated. Actually, the issue of our time, perhaps the issue of all human time, is which of the two outputs will prevail.

Too much these days we forget that men's ability to control the physical depends upon the moral. Nothing that statesmen can contrive will work if it does not reflect the moral conscience of the time. Whenever that limitation is ignored, failure ensues. We need to recall that now when many are panicky and demand something that, on paper at least, will seem to give them security. . . . When war occurs, nations avail themselves of any weapon which they think will make the difference between victory and defeat. No agreements are allowed to stand in the way. Indeed, nations at war would consider such self-restraint to be morally wrong. For in war, nations always identify their cause with righteousness and identify the enemy with the forces of evil. Thus, until govern-

Address delivered on the occasion of the inauguration of the President of Union Theological Seminary, November 15, 1945, and repeated in condensed form to the Board of Directors of Union Seminary on May 27, 1958.

ments take a totally different conception of the moral sanctity of contracts in time of war, it is folly to believe that the destructiveness of war can be limited by agreements not to use certain weapons. . . .

The task of statesmanship is to relate theory to reality. Political institutions ought to be as perfect as is consonant with their vigorous survival in the existing environment. Also, of course, those institutions ought to contain within themselves the possibility of improving the environment and thereby making more perfection possible. The United Nations Charter has that great merit. It does not accept as permanent the existing distrusts. It charges the nations, under the leadership of the General Assembly, to work together on tasks of human welfare. The assumption, and the reasonable assumption, is that if they do that, fellowship between nations will grow.

The central problem is how to get world law. Once we can agree upon a lawmaking body, then it will be possible to put overwhelming force behind it. However, it is not possible to have a lawmaking body until there is greater trust and confidence between the peoples of the world, until there is more widespread acceptance and practice of democratic methods, and until there is more nearly a common moral judgment of what is right and wrong.

There is no political short cut to the safety men want. We must carry through the program of San Francisco. We must use the United Nations Organization to bring about that greater trust and fellowship we need before we can have any world government that will work. Fellowship, and not fear, is the cement with which world order must be built. The urgent task is to increase that fellowship and not to abandon that effort on the ground that increased fear makes it unnecessary.

I realize that such a program as I here outline will not satisfy the many who are panicky and the many who are impatient. They want to be shown a formula for quick and absolute security. It would be easy to write one. It would be impossible to write one that would work. There is no short cut. There is no mechanistic solution. It is not possible by a stroke of the pen to make up for accumulated moral deficiencies. What is possible is to increase steadily the acceptance and practice of the moral law. If we do that, then many other things will become possible.

When I talk along this line, it is often replied that I am impractical and idealistic and that we cannot wait for results until the whole world has become evangelized or at least has become highly moral. Such comment merely shows that I have failed to make my meaning clear. To rely upon the force of the moral law is the most practical thing in the world today. It is general acceptance of moral law which gives us 99 per cent of the practical security which we enjoy. It is where the moral law is weakest in its application, namely, in relation to bodies corporate, that the greatest danger comes. There is nothing impractical about attempting to extend the system which practically gives us protection. On the contrary, what is impractical and unrealistic is to depend upon agreements by governments which have no moral sanction behind them. . . .

To seek to extend the rule of the moral law . . . is not a program which will be without results until the millennium is achieved. The most important protection we can get comes, not from where we are, but from the way in which we are moving. If the postwar trend is toward increased fellowship and increasing trust and confidence, then that itself will bring us a large measure of protection as a by-product. So long as the trend is in that direction, nations do not interrupt it to wipe each other out with atomic bombs. It is when the trend is toward increased distrust that we need to be afraid.

We can, therefore, with confidence assert that a peaceful order depends most of all upon intensive use of those methods which have been tried and which have worked in the past. Of those methods, the most successful has been extension of the moral law, and in bringing the people to act toward each other in fellowship and as good neighbors. We must not allow ourselves to be diverted from pushing forward along that line. In that effort our greatest reliance is, of course, upon the great religious bodies of the world. It is they, above all others, which create the moral foundation which, in turn, determines the political structure which can be built. These religious bodies, in turn, are dependent upon their seminaries. So it is that the great theological seminaries, of which Union Theological Seminary is an outstanding example, are in reality the central power plants upon which men must, above all, depend not merely for their spiritual salvation but for their material safety.

V

The Power of Moral Forces

This collection began with an address delivered by Mr. Dulles on August 28, 1949, in the First Presbyterian Church of Watertown, New York, in which he had worshiped throughout his boyhood under his father's ministry.

On October 11, 1953, he returned to Watertown to take part in the celebration of the one hundred and fiftieth anniversary of the church. The address delivered on that occasion gathers into summary many of the central convictions of his life.

22

The Power of Moral Forces

I⟨T WAS⟩ nearly two years ago that your minister asked me to come here to speak at this one hundred and fiftieth anniversary of the founding of our church. I accepted that invitation. Since then I have had to make and unmake many plans. But this date has been a fixed point around which other things revolved.

I have looked forward eagerly to being here on this historic occasion. It rightfully means much to all of you here and to this entire area. To me this church is richer in memories than any other earthly spot. My father preached here for sixteen years and radiated a spiritual influence that is still felt here, and elsewhere, as I have learned in my travels about the world. Our family life revolved around this church. Before me is the pew in which we sat three times on Sunday and frequently during weekday evenings.

At times the church services seemed overlong and over-frequent. But through them I was taught of the two great commandments, love of God and love of fellow man. Ordained

Address delivered at the Interdenominational Community Service celebrating the one hundred and fiftieth anniversary of the First Presbyterian Church, Watertown, New York, October 11, 1953.

ministers are uniquely qualified to deal with the relations of man to God. But laymen, who have to deal with national and international problems, are perhaps qualified to make some observations on the relations of man to fellow man.

Let me first recall that our American political institutions are what they are because our founders were deeply religious people. As soon as a community was founded, a church was built. This church is an example. Also, wherever a community was founded, its members developed practices and ways of life which reflected their belief that there is a God, that he is the author of a moral law which all can know and should obey, that he imparts to each human being a spiritual dignity and worth which all should respect.

Our founders sought to reflect these truths in their political institutions, seeking thus that God's will should be done on earth.

The Bill of Rights puts into our supreme law the concept "that all men are endowed by their Creator with certain inalienable rights." Our Constitution says, in unmistakable terms, that men, even in the guise of government, cannot lawfully deny other men their fundamental rights and freedoms.

From the beginning of our nation, those who made its laws and system of justice looked upon them as means to assure what seemed just and right. Thus we became heirs to a noble heritage.

We must, however, remember that that heritage is not inexhaustible. Our institutions of freedom will not survive unless they are constantly replenished by the faith that gave them birth.

General Washington, in his Farewell Address, pointed out that morality and religion are the two pillars of our society. He went on to say that morality cannot be maintained without religion. "Whatever may be conceded to the influence of refined education on minds of peculiar structure, reason and experience both forbid us to expect that national morality can prevail in exclusion of religious principle."

Arnold Toynbee, the great student of civilizations, has recently pointed out that the political and social practices of our civilization derive from their Christian content, and, he says, they will not long survive unless they are replenished by that faith. His profound study convinces him that "practice unsupported by belief is a wasting asset."

Many other nations have modeled their constitutions after ours. But they have not obtained the same results unless there was a faith to vitalize the words.

The terrible things that are happening in some parts of the world are due to the fact that political and social practices have been separated from spiritual content.

That separation is almost total in the Soviet Communist world. There the rulers hold a materialistic creed which denies the existence of moral law. It denies that men are spiritual beings. It denies that there are any such things as eternal verities. As a result the Soviet institutions treat human beings as primarily important from the standpoint of how much they can be made to produce for the glorification of the state. Labor is essentially slave labor, working to build up the military and material might of the state so that those who rule can assert ever greater and more frightening power.

Such conditions repel us. But it is important to understand what causes those conditions. It is irreligion. If ever the political forces in this country became irreligious, our institutions would change. The change might come about slowly, but it would come surely. Institutions born of faith will inevitably change unless they are constantly nurtured by faith.

But, it may be asked, may not aggressive material forces prevail unless met by materialism? It sometimes seems that material power is so potent that it should be sought at any price, even at the sacrifice of spiritual values. Always, however, in the past those who took that path have met disaster. Material aggression often is formidable. It is dynamic, and we must admit that the dynamic usually prevails over the static. But it is gross error to assume that material forces have a monopoly of dynamism. Moral forces too are mighty. Christians, to be sure, do not believe in invoking brute power to secure their ends. But that does not mean that they have no ends or that they have no means of getting there. Christians are not negative, supine people.

Jesus told the disciples to go out into all the world and to preach the gospel to all the nations. Any nation which bases its institutions on Christian principles cannot but be a dynamic nation.

Our forebears felt keenly that this nation had a mission to perform. In the opening paragraph of *The Federalist* papers it is said that "it seems to have been reserved to the people of this country, by their conduct and example," to show the way to political freedom. Our Declaration of Independence meant, as Lincoln said, "liberty, not alone to the people of this country but hope for the world for all future time. It was that which gave promise that in due time the weight should be lifted from the shoulders of all men and that all should have an equal chance."

What our forebears did became known as "the great American experiment." They created here a society of material, intellectual, and spiritual richness the like of which the world had never known. It was not selfishly designed, but for ourselves and others. We sought through conduct, example, and influence to promote everywhere the cause of human freedom. Through missionaries, physicians, educators, and merchants, the American people carried their ideas and ideals to others. They availed of every opportunity to spread their gospel of freedom, their good news, throughout the world.

That performance so caught the imagination of the peoples of the world that everywhere men wanted for themselves a political freedom which could bear such fruits.

The despotisms of the last century faded away largely under the influence of that conduct and example. There is no despotism in the world which can stand up against the impact of such a gospel. That needs to be remembered today. Our best reliance is not more and bigger bombs but a way of life which reflects religious faith.

Do our people still have that faith which in the past made our nation truly great and which we need today? That is the ultimate testing of our time. Admittedly, some have come to think primarily in material terms. They calculate the atomic stockpiles, the bombers, the tanks, the standing armies of the various nations, and seem to assume that the victory will go to whichever is shown by these scales to have the greater weight of armament.

Unfortunately, under present conditions we do need to have a strong military establishment. We are opposed by those who respect only visible strength and who are tempted to encroach where there seems to be material weakness. Therefore, without military strength, we could not expect to deter aggression which, even though it would ultimately fail, would in the process cause immense misery and loss. But I can assure you that your Government does not put its faith primarily in material things.

The greatest weakness of our opponents is that they are professed materialists. They have forcibly extended their rule over some eight hundred million people, a third of the people of the world. They are seeking to make these people into a pliant, physical mass which completely conforms to the will of the rulers. But these people are religious people and they are patriotic people. They have shown that over the centuries. We believe that the Soviet rulers are attempting the impossible when they attempt to subject such people to their materialistic and repressive rule. We believe that the subject peoples have faith and hopes which cannot indefinitely be suppressed.

I can assure you that your President, your Cabinet, your Congress, recognize the priority of spiritual forces. We do not intend to turn this nation into a purely material fortress and to suppress the freedom of thought and expression of the inmates, so that our people would more and more assume the likeness of that which threatens and which we hate.

There are a few within this nation who do not share their viewpoint. They honestly feel that the danger is so great and of such a kind that we must give an absolute priority to material efforts. There are others who honestly feel that the danger is so imminent that we should impose uniformity of thought, or at least of expression, abolishing diversity and tolerance within our nation and within our alliances.

Such points of view, while often heard, represent a small minority. Certainly there is some confusion of thinking, which needs to be dispelled. But I believe that the great majority of the American people and of their representatives in Government still accept the words of the prophet: "Not by might, nor by power, but by my Spirit, saith the Lord of hosts."

How shall we surely become infused with that spirit? That is my concluding concern.

There is no mystery about that. The way to get faith is to expose oneself to the faith of others. It is not only diseases that are contagious. Faith is contagious. A strong faith, rooted in fact and in reason, inevitably spreads if contacts are provided. If, therefore, we want spiritual strength, we must maintain contact with those who have it and with those who have had it.

That is above all the task of our churches. The Bible is the greatest book because, as Paul pointed out to the Hebrews, it is a story of faith. It recounts lapses from faith and their consequences, and revival and restoration of faith. Most of all, it is a story of men who lived by faith and died in faith, bequeathing it to successors who molded it into something finer, truer, and more worthy.

Our American history, like Hebrew history, is also rich in the story of men who through faith wrought mightily.

In earlier days our homes, schools, and colleges were largely consecrated to the development of faith. They were places of prayer and of Bible-reading. Parents and teachers told daily the story of those who had gone before and who had lived by faith.

Today our schools and colleges and, I am afraid, our homes largely omit this study in faith. That throws a heavier burden on our churches. They today provide the principal means of drawing together the men, women, and children of our land and of bringing to them knowledge of the faith of those who have gone before, so that today's faith is a contagious and vital force.

As our churches, synagogues, and other places of worship thus carry an ever-greater share of vital responsibility, they should be strongly supported by all our citizens, for they all profit from the institutions which faith inspires.

As we meet here today on this anniversary, we feel that we are indeed compassed about by a great crowd of witnesses. Each of us here knows that in terms of loved ones who have gone before. We know it as we have heard read here the great Book of Faith and as we are taught here the lessons drawn from the story of the great prophets and disciples of the past.

Let us maintain spiritual communion with them. Let us draw faith and inspiration from their lives. Let us act as we know they would want us to act. Then we, in our turn, will run with steadfastness the course that is set before us. Then we, in our turn, will play worthily our part in keeping alight the flame of freedom.

I spoke earlier of the spiritual legacy that had been left us by our fathers. Surely it is our duty not to squander it but to leave it replenished so that we, in our generation, may bequeath to those who come after us a tradition as noble as was left to us.

We meet here beneath a spire which is symbolic. It points upward to the Power above us, from which we derive our spiritual strength. It marks this building as the place where we can gather for a communion that renews our faith.

Let us be ever thankful for this church, remembering those who a century and a half ago founded it. Let us remember also those who during the succeeding decades maintained it, enlarged it, beautified it, and enriched it with their Christian labors. Let us dedicate ourselves to follow in their way.

John Foster Dulles

BORN: February 25, 1888, Washington, D.C.

PARENTS: Allen Macy and Edith (Foster) Dulles

WIFE: Janet Pomery Avery, married June 26, 1912

CHILDREN: John Watson Foster, Lillias Pomeroy (Mrs. Robert Hinshaw), Avery

DIED: May 24, 1959

Academic Record

B.A., *magna cum laude* Princeton University, 1908, Valedictorian

Studied at the Sorbonne, Paris, 1908–1909

LL.B., George Washington University, 1911

LL.D., Tufts, 1939; Princeton University, 1946; Wagner College, Northwestern University, 1947; Union College, 1948; University of Pennsylvania, Lafayette, 1949; Amherst, Seoul National University, 1950; University of Arizona, St. Joseph's College, 1951; St. Lawrence University, Johns Hopkins University, Fordham University, Harvard, 1952; Columbia University, Georgetown University, 1954; University of South Carolina, Indiana University, 1955; Iowa State University, 1956.

Career in National and International Affairs

Secretary of The Hague Peace Conference, 1907

Member of the Second Pan-American Scientific Congress

Special Agent, Department of State, in Central America, 1917

Captain and Major, U.S. Army (Intelligence), 1917–1918

Assistant to Chairman, War Trade Board, 1918

Counsel to American Commission to Negotiate Peace, 1918–1919

Member, Reparations Commission and Supreme Economic Council, 1919

Legal Adviser, Polish plan of financial stabilization, 1927

American Representative, Berlin debt conferences, 1933

Member, U.S. delegation, San Francisco Conference on World Organization, 1945, United Nations General Assembly, 1946, 1947, 1950.

Acting Chairman, U.S. delegation, UN General Assembly, Paris, 1948

Adviser to Secretary of State at Council of Foreign Ministers, London, 1945, 1947; Moscow, 1947; Paris, 1949

United States Senator, appointed 1949

Consultant to Secretary of State, 1950

Special representative of President, with rank of ambassador, negotiated Japanese Peace Treaty, 1951

Negotiator of Australian, New Zealand, Philippine, and Japanese Security Treaties, 1950–1951

Secretary of State, 1953–1959

Special Consultant to the President, 1959

Affiliations

Member, Sullivan & Cromwell, attorneys, 1911–1949; head of firm, 1927–1949

Chairman, Board of Trustees, Rockefeller Foundation, Carnegie Endowment for International Peace, General Education Board

Trustee, Bank of New York, New York Public Library

Member, Association of the Bar of the City of New York, New York State Banking Board, Phi Beta Kappa, Phi Delta Phi

Church Relationships

Member, First Presbyterian Church, Watertown, New York, baptized July 1, 1888; received on profession of faith to communicant membership, July 5, 1902

Elder, Park Avenue Presbyterian Church, New York City; Brick Presbyterian Church, New York City, 1937–1959

Delegate, Conference on Church, Community, and State, Oxford, 1937

Delegate, International Conference of Lay Experts and Ecumenical Leaders, convened by the Provisional Committee of the World Council of Churches, Geneva, 1939

Chairman, Commission to Study the Bases of a Just and Durable Peace, Federal Council of the Churches of Christ in America, 1940–1948

Chairman, Committee on Policy, Department of International Justice and Goodwill, 1948–1949; Member of the department, 1951–1952

Director, Union Theological Seminary, New York City, 1945–1953

Member, Commission of the Churches on International Affairs, 1947–1953

Author, statement on "The Christian Citizen in a Changing World" in preparation for the first Assembly of the World Council of Churches, Amsterdam, 1948

Speaker, first Assembly of the World Council of Churches,
Amsterdam, 1948

Books

War, Peace and Change, 1939
War or Peace, 1950